Nonfiction Writing Strategies

Using Content-Area Mentor Texts

Marcia S. Freeman

Maupin House by
capstone·
professional

Nonfiction Writing Strategies
Using Content-Area Mentor Texts
By Marcia S. Freeman

Cover Design: Sarah Bennett

Book Design: Jodi Pedersen

Library of Congress Cataloging-in-Publication Data
Cataloging-in-publication information is on file with the Library of Congress.
ISBN-13: 978-1-62521-512-3

Maupin House publishes professional resources for K–12 educators. Contact us for tailored, in-school training or to schedule an author for a workshop or conference. Visit www.maupinhouse.com for free lesson plan downloads.

Maupin House Publishing, Inc. by Capstone Professional
1710 Roe Crest Drive
North Mankato, MN 56003
www.maupinhouse.com
888-262-6135
info@maupinhouse.com

Printed in the United States of America in Eau Claire, Wisconsin.
122013   007924

Contents

Dedication

In memory of Dr. Richard B. Fischer and Dr. Verne N. Rockcastle,
Professors Emeritus, Science and Environmental Education
Cornell University

Preface

One of the basic tenets of all my writing education work—my texts *Building a Writing Community: A Practical Guide, Teaching the Youngest Writers, Listen to This: Developing an Ear for Expository,* and my K–8 writing program, *CraftPlus*—is that writing is a craft and we must teach students how to use that craft to create lively, people-oriented, engaging expository prose.

In my texts and in *CraftPlus* I provide an array of techniques, such as organization schemes, beginnings and endings, literary devices, and ways to engage the reader. I show how, in the context of classroom daily writing workshops, we can model these techniques—something we need to do again and again. In our modeling we show students how professional writers use particular craft skills. We then invite young writers to emulate "the pros" and we show them how to do it. Finally, we reward and encourage them as they attempt to apply these skills in their own writing.

In this manner we can turn our students into eager, knowledgeable, and competent writers. Teachers who use my instructional texts and apply this approach proudly show me the high-quality informational writing their young students have done in response to the craft-skill models and lessons. These students, and the ones I teach, love to show me magazines and books and exclaim, "Look, Mrs. Freeman, this author did the same thing we do!" This is positive proof that young writers can and do learn and apply the techniques that support and nurture their natural informational writing mode.

When teaching young students the writing craft, I have found using photo-illustrated informational texts an effective way to model the craft skills that creative nonfiction authors use. In primary grades, the content-area Shared Reading Texts are especially useful. Use them for shared reading experiences for their content and then in writing instruction lessons for the specific craft skills they illustrate. The intent of this book is to encourage you to use a variety of nonfiction mentor texts in your classroom after you have used them for their content. At that point, the text will be familiar to your students, and they will be able to look beyond the books' contents to observe the wonderful writing craft they contain. Of course, you can and should use any other well-written expository texts.

Please note that the lessons described in this book are effective for kindergarten to fourth-grade students. In third and fourth grade, most students can read the books by themselves. I recommend that third and fourth grade teachers borrow informational science and social studies books from primary colleagues and use and enjoy the books for both their information and their writing-craft content.

Marcia S. Freeman

Acknowledgments

Special thanks to Luana Mitten, Mary Beth Laiti, Michelle Figga Burgroff, and their primary students at Dunbar Elementary School, Tampa, Florida, who generously donated many of their class charts and practice pieces to show the world what young writers can do when instructed in writing craft.

Marcia S. Freeman

Introduction

If you think about it, almost everything we write throughout our lives is expository—writing to inform, explain, describe, propose, amuse, remind, direct, teach, and persuade. Students need to master the expository genre for academic success and, subsequently, job success.

In working toward this mastery they need to hear and analyze models of good expository writing. Yet, when we read to children we tend to choose stories. We overuse and misuse the term *story*. We refer to young children's writing as *story*, as in, "Bring your *story* to Author's Chair." "Read your *story* to me." "Tell me about your *story*."

We do this regardless of whether the writing is a story. For example, a typical first grader's piece—*I love my dog. He plays with me. He licks my face and it feels soft.*—is not a story; it is an informational expository piece.

We ask students to write stories in response to the stories we read to them. We even ask them to write stories in response to science and social studies text and study. Such responses should not be stories; they should be expository writing that includes description, information, comparison, and opinion.

Ironically, the natural writing mode of primary-grade writers *is* expository. They love to tell what they know and how they feel. And in fact, few children, until mid to late first grade, are able to put events in a time sequence, which is the basic requirement of story writing.

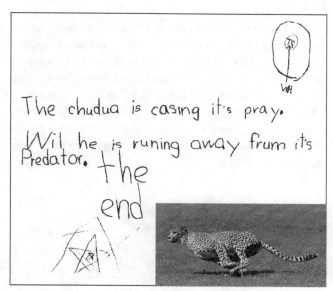

Grade 1

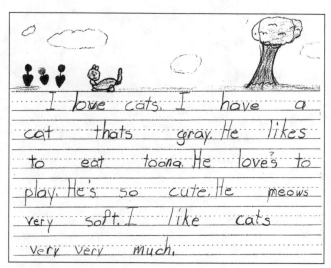

Grade 1

Supporting Children's Natural Writing Mode

We need to support and nurture our young writers' natural writing mode by reading them lively, graceful, informational texts and by teaching them appropriate techniques to use as they write about what they know and feel.

This book will show you how to use Capstone nonfiction mentor texts to help you teach and model grade-appropriate informational writing skills, meeting both Common Core State Standards and Next Generation Science Standards. The nonfiction texts chosen are an effective aid in this regard because, in addition to their informational content, they provide examples of the craft techniques young writers can apply to their own nonfiction writing.

More About Expository Writing

Writing about facts and describing objects, scenes, and processes is the simplest expository form. From there, the genre progresses to the more abstract task of writing about ideas and opinions, i.e., essay.

Piaget tells us that children in the early elementary grades, ages 5 to 10, are in the concrete-operational stage. Around the age of 10 they begin to move into the abstract or formal thinking stage, although many do not make that move until several years later. Thus, writing about facts or information—describing and explaining—is the expository writing that elementary students are capable of and thrive on. It is exactly the kind of writing you will find in Capstone mentor texts.

How to Use This Book

Each of the subsequent chapters of this book deals with an aspect of the writing craft that young writers—kindergarten through fourth grade—can use and for which Capstone content-area, informational books provide excellent models. Very often, a Shared Reading Text (SRT) is the best choice for elementary students at any grade level. Books available as larger Shared Reading Texts are noted in each list with (SRT). Each chapter describes lessons pertaining to writing craft. The lessons are accompanied by a list of specific books that contain excellent models of the craft skill under study. Some of the lessons described in the book utilize pictures as well as mentor texts.

I recommend that you use the books you select for their illustrative text for writing lessons *after* you and your students have enjoyed them in shared reading experiences and after using them for their subject content. Once the students are familiar with the pictures and text they will be able to concentrate on the writing-craft lesson model you present.

How to Teach a Writing-Craft Skill

An important principle in teaching children the writing craft is to show them how accomplished writers use a particular skill and to encourage them to emulate those writers. I have found that the most effective way to apply this principle is to use the following steps.

Introduce the Concept (Awareness)
- Introduce a skill by pointing out examples in the mentor text selected and,
- Talk about the skill—what did the author do to make the writing clear, interesting, or pleasant sounding?

Models from Books
- Share other nonfiction texts that illustrate the skill.

Try It Out Orally
- Model the skill orally for students.
- Have the children try it out orally.

Try It Out in Writing
- Demonstrate the technique through **shared writing**.
- Demonstrate the technique through **modeled writing**—thinking aloud as you compose in front of your students. (Prepare your models beforehand.)

Practice and Application
- Help the children try out the skill in a small practice piece or in guided writing.
- Provide opportunities for students to practice the skill in their **independent writing**.

Assessment
- Call for and assess the use of the skill in a piece of writing.

Shared Writing Tip

Shared writing should be conducted within a limited time frame. If a session goes on too long, young students lose interest and start to fidget. One way to keep within a time frame that fits your students' attention spans is to limit the contributions to selected students. Use a rotating schedule to ensure that, over time, every student gets to participate.

The first seven steps in teaching a craft skill are instructive in nature. Use them as starting components in your daily writing workshop. In kindergarten and first grade, you might do the oral components over one or two days and follow with the written component, through shared or modeled writing, on a subsequent day.

In second through fourth grades, you might combine the oral components with the students' first attempts to use the skill in a small written piece on the same day. This piece should be purely for practice. Check only to see if your students are able to use the skill.

> ### Practice Writing
> Most (about 80 percent) of the writing students do in daily writing workshop should be pure practice. Think of learning to write as analogous to learning a musical instrument. Practice sessions consist of working on skills, then working through a piece in which those skills are applied. Practice pieces are not evaluated; they are guided and encouraged. After ample practice, a developed piece is taken through the entire writing process (from prewriting to editing) and presented for evaluation.

Models

You will need to prepare the lesson models you perform for students, whether the models are oral or written. Prepare them carefully so that they are short (three to five sentences, depending on your students' attention spans), clear, and interesting illustrations of the skill. When you use them in modeled writing, think aloud as you compose, presenting them as if you were making them up on the spot.

By always talking or writing three or more related sentences about a picture or topic when you model, you will safeguard against **Single-Sentence Syndrome,** the caption-writing disease many young writers suffer. We inadvertently promote this syndrome by modeling it in the primary grades. Young writers need to learn early that their ideas should be developed.

Design some models so that your second, third, and fourth graders can write in tandem with you, sentence by sentence, creating their versions of the piece you model. They will be more actively involved. See page 59 for a description of tandem writing.

Use your models repetitively, continually modifying and advancing them as your students grow in their ability to understand and use the modeled skill.

Student Writing as Models

Student samples are powerful models in writing workshop. The children see what other young writers their age can do and they see that you value student writing as highly as you do professional writing.

Collect student samples from former classes of your own or from colleagues' classes at your grade level. Be sure to get permission from your young writers to use their work as models.

Goals

In some craft lessons, your goal will be simple awareness and recognition of the craft skill, or oral usage. In others, your goal will be students' application or attempted application in writing. The choice will be determined by your young writers' current experience and fluency level.

In a well-constructed, schoolwide writing program, young writers get to see the same writing-craft skills modeled with increasing sophistication as they progress through the grades. Even with ample practice, it can take several months or even years for them to learn to use a skill fluently and gracefully. They increase their knowledge of the craft by seeing the skills they are studying used in printed text. Continually encouraged by us, they will learn to write by mimicking the pros.

Professional Literature

As with any subject, your ability to teach writing depends on your knowledge and experience with it. Many of us leave high school and college with a high level of anxiety about our writing, particularly expository writing, and do not feel confident to teach it. It behooves us, therefore, to read professionally and learn about the techniques we can teach our young students.

For practical information about teaching craft skills, modeling and sharing techniques, and managing a classroom daily writing workshop I refer you to my teacher's textbooks: *Listen to This: Developing an Ear for Expository, Building a Writing Community: A Practical*

Guide, and *Teaching the Youngest Writers.* Additionally, I highly recommend authors William Zinsser and Gary Provost for information about the writing craft (see Bibliography).

Target Skills

Target Skills are the writing-craft techniques you will teach your young writers during the year. They are the skills the children will practice. And they are the skills you will assess after students have had ample opportunity to practice.

The Target Skill lessons featured in this book can be applied in kindergarten through fourth grade. Primary-grade, nonfiction books and Shared Reading Texts make great models for older students as they can read the text easily and can readily see the writing-craft skills used to present the content.

How This Book Is Organized

In the first chapter, I describe the Target Skill concept and modeling. In each of the subsequent four chapters, I treat a variety of specific informational writing techniques and describe lessons about them for the different grade levels.

The techniques include the following:
- Organization Schemes for Informational Writing
- Composing Skills
- Beginnings
- Endings

I devote one chapter to showing how to use photographs to prepare students for performance-based comprehensive assessment test writing.

The techniques include the following:
- Supporting Details
- Presenting Information Graphically

The final chapter describes using Shared Reading Texts and nonfiction mentor texts to teach young writers how to edit for several kinds of punctuation.

CHAPTER 1: **The Target Skill**

If children write often, they will gain mechanical fluency, and that is a significant primary-grade goal. But writing every day does not necessarily engender composing fluency, facility with *real writing skills* like organizing, composing, elaborating, and using conventions. For students to achieve composing fluency, they must learn and practice the content of writing—the body of knowledge that defines the craft.

That body of knowledge consists of specific techniques from three general categories:

- organization (example: clumping related facts in an informational piece)
- composing and literary devices (example: using strong verbs and comparisons)
- writing conventions (example: starting a sentence with a capital letter)

I call these techniques and conventions **Target Skills.** They are the skills you must teach in daily writing workshop to ensure advances in the quality of your students' writing. You do this through modeling and direct instruction.

Kindergarten students can be introduced to writing craft as soon as they enter school. They are able to *talk* the Target Skill even though they may not be able to put it in writing. For example, you can show them the difference between strong-verb writing and static writing, *The boy is climbing a tree* versus *There is a boy.* They can talk about their drawings or photographs by telling what is *happening* rather than telling *what is.*

In **grades two through four,** Target Skills are introduced, practiced, and assessed over the course of several weeks. You should present the skills as they relate to the specific genre your students may do during a two- to three-week period. Over a school year, you would revisit some skills several times as the writing form (connected to thematic units, projects, and literature study) changes.

For example, in a second-grade class, you might introduce *using comparisons* as a Target Skill during the first weeks of school when you are focusing on descriptive writing to develop some fluency while you establish writing workshop procedures. You might then revisit *using comparisons* as a Target Skill for a science informational piece later in the year.

The Picture-Prompted Writing Model

A picture-prompted writing model is a handy way to introduce the Target Skill concept in all grades. In the model you use a photograph or a Shared Reading Text cover to trigger discussion and subsequent writing. Visual perception is a dominant learning mode in humans and is becoming even more so in the age of TV and computer icons and symbols. Photographs help students who might be inclined to say, "I don't know what to write about."

A photograph is a concrete aid: Children can hold it, feel it, and talk about it. Show them how to choose pictures that match their personal experiences and interests.

Modeling the Picture-Prompted Target Skill Process for the First Time (grades K–4)

The process you will model consists of selecting a picture, talking about it, and writing about it. The process takes two blocks of time: one for the selection and talking and one for the writing. Early-stage emergent writers can do this all orally, as a whole-class sharing activity and again with partners.

For your model, you will need a large collection of colorful pictures. The collection should include children engaged in play, work, sports, eating, etc.; insects, birds, reptiles, mammals, fish, etc.; rural and urban scenes; and so on. Ask parents, friends, neighbors, and relatives to collect color pictures for your class. *National Geographic* magazines are a wonderful source, and you can often find them at garage sales or used bookstores. Laminate the pictures or place them in plastic covers.

Commercial photo cards are also an excellent resource for picture-prompted writing. They are laminated and students can write on them with washable pens. Children often use the discussion questions and other text on the back to help spell words associated with the picture.

- Emergent writers might use the starting letters of words to label things they see in the photos. They can tell what is happening rather than saying what things are. They can talk about where things are as they study the concepts of up/down, over/under, near/far, in/out, etc.

- ESOL students might work with English-speaking students and write the names of things they identify directly on the cards.

The modeling process for picture-prompted Target Skill writing has four steps. In kindergarten and first grade the sequence may take several days. In second, third, and fourth grades, you might do steps 1, 2, and 4 on one day and steps 2, 3, and 4 on a subsequent day.

Step 1: Model Picture Selection

Gather your class at the easel or meeting place. Display an assortment of pictures. Tell the children you are going to select a picture to talk and write about. Think aloud as you make your selection. *Maybe I will write about this picture. It looks just like my dog: same color, same floppy ears.* Or *I could do this one: I love fire engines. There is a firehouse on the way to school and I always slow down to see the engines.* Or *This picture makes me feel happy. It reminds me of my brother, and how we often go fishing together in a rowboat.*

Place groups of pictures on tables around the room and invite the children to browse, just as if they were in a library looking for a book. Invite them to select a picture. Suggest that they look for a picture about **something they know**, or **something they can do**, or **a place where they might have been**—a topic related to their

personal background and experience. If two students want the same picture, settle the issue quickly with a coin toss.

Gather your young writers again and give them five minutes to talk about their pictures in partnerships or small groups.

Laminated Picture Collection

Write several key words, nouns and verbs that relate to the pictures on the back of the mounted pictures before you laminate them. Young writers can then use the words for spelling help when they write about them.

When you introduce your students to the cards tell them the words on the back are *content words*. Your class editing standards in grade two and above should require that young writers be responsible for the correct spelling of content words when they write on a topic.

Back of card

rowboat
lifting
shore
rock
pebbles

Step 2: Model Talking About the Picture to Introduce the Target Skill

A. Kindergarten and First-Grade Model

Gather your students to the meeting place. Have them sit in a circle facing you. Ask them to sit on their pictures. Place your photo on the easel. Tell them, "We are going to talk about our pictures and later we are going to write about them."

Show your students the difference between "Dinky Writing" and "Good Writing." (*Dinky* is akin to *Stinky* and the children are amused by that; subsequently, they remember it.) Illustrate "Dinky Writing" by talking about your picture, saying such things as: *There is a boy. It is sunny. There is a wagon.* Tell the children to give a *thumbs-down* for "Dinky Writing." Illustrate *thumbs-down*. (The signal is silent but it employs movement.)

Tell them that readers like to learn about what is going on. Now talk about the photo, saying such things as: *The boy is pulling a wagon. The sun is shining down on his head. The boy in the back of the wagon is pushing.* Ask your students to give a *thumbs-up* for good writing. (The emphasis is on verbs.)

Invite each child, in turn, to tell **what is happening** in his or her picture. Help students along by modeling again between some of their responses. Have listeners give *thumbs-up* for good writing (even though it is only good *talking* at this stage).

Send children back to their tables or desks and invite them to write about their pictures as you continue writing workshop. Rove and encourage. Remind them to tell **what is happening** but do not say anything if they do not. Note the children who try to tell what is happening, orally or in drawing/written form. Conduct a sharing session either through Author's Chair or by having every young writer "read" his or her work to another young writer before putting it away.

Shared Writing

In the following day's writing workshop, gather your students to the meeting place. Place a piece of chart paper on the easel or use a whiteboard and markers. Display a Shared Reading Text cover or a large picture. Draw a little bull's-eye target in the right-hand corner of the paper or board. Tell your young writers, "That target reminds us to tell our readers **what is happening** when we write about our picture."

Now, ask your students to compose a description of a picture using the Target Skill. Write the sentences offered by students. (Devise a record-keeping system that ensures every student gets a turn at supplying sentences in your shared writing sessions. You might consider a rotating system wherein selected students get to contribute each day.) I add children's initials in the margin opposite the contributions they make to a class piece. Later they point out their contributions to each other. "Look, that's what I said."

Again, in the continuation of the writing workshop, invite students to write about their pictures using the Target Skill, *what is happening*, and to share their work with another writer. Rove and encourage. The resulting independent writing will run the gamut of drawings, scribbles, random letters, single consonant strings, letter strings with a letter-to-word correspondence, decipherable writing of transitional spelling—that is, the typical range of emergent to developing writing that a class of primary students demonstrates.

B. Mid-First Grade through Fourth Grade

When all students have selected a picture, ask them to place their pictures on their desks and come to the meeting place. On the class easel, place or draw a picture of an archery target labeled **TARGET** with an arrow drawn in the bull's-eye.

Ask a child who you know is articulate to be your partner. Tell the children that you and your partner are going to model a "knee-to-knee" writer's conference about the pictures.

Teacher: Writers try very hard to help you, their reader, see what they see, know what they know. They make sure they tell what the people or animals are doing, what is happening, what colors, numbers, shapes, and sizes you would want to know about. Today, I would like you to tell what is happening in your picture when you describe your picture to your partner. That will be what you **aim** for when you talk and write about your picture. That will be your **TARGET**. Point to the target picture. Watch Jennifer and me as we try to hit the **TARGET**.

(Sit across from Jennifer, knee-to-knee, and begin.)

Teacher: The target is to tell what is happening in the picture. I will try to do that. Jennifer, I picked this picture because I love dogs. I have one just like this. The two children are pulling on the dog's collar, trying to slow him down. He's so big, he is pulling them. He's tan, like the color of a football. (Pause.) Did I hit the target? What did you hear me say was happening?

Jennifer: I heard you say the dog is *pulling* the kids.

Another student: And you said the kids are *pulling* on the collar.

Teacher: Good job hearing if I hit the target. Now it is Jennifer's turn.

Jennifer: My picture is a little girl *pushing* her sister in a swing. Did I hit the target?

Teacher: Yes, you did. And, you can tell anything else you like about your picture.

Jennifer: She looks like she likes it.

Teacher: How did you know that?

Jennifer: She is *smiling*.

Teacher: Thank you for conferencing with me. Boys and girls, you are all going to conference with your partners now. Will you try to hit the **TARGET,** telling *what* is *happening* in the picture? Remember, you can say anything about picture, but do try to tell your partner what is happening in the picture. Aim for the target.

Write: *What is happening?* next to the target on the easel or board.

Begin student knee-to-knee prewriting conferences. You may gather some young writers who you know cannot do peer conferencing on their own to work with you in a group. Encourage them to tell the group what is happening in their pictures. Invite the members of the group to give a silent, thumbs-up signal when they think they hear the writer hit the target—when they hear *what is happening* in the picture. Model your picture description again, using a different verb phrase than you did in your first model.

Sharing

When the children have finished conferencing (five minutes is usually sufficient), use the sharing technique of asking young writers to compliment their partners: *Who heard their partners hit the target? Please tell us your partners' names and what they said was happening?* Listen to several children's examples. Sharing in this fashion is critical for the development of your classroom writing community.

- Young writers will have to pay close attention as their partners read—this fosters listening skills.

- Young writers will be broadcasting examples of their partners' good ideas—this contributes to the pool of writing knowledge.

- Two students are rewarded at the same time; the writer and the listener—this uses time efficiently.

- Peers will be giving compliments for achievement—this builds respect and a sense of community.

- You will not be the sole source of compliments—this fosters independence.

Step 3: Model Writing to the Target Skill

At the start of the next day's writing workshop gather your students to the easel where you have placed your picture and paper. Draw a little archery target in the upper right-hand corner. Tell your young writers, "This stands for the **Target Skill.** Who remembers yesterday's target? That's right, it was: *What is happening?*" Write an H under the target. Say, "H stands for happening."

Under your picture, write a sentence that tells what is happening. *The kids are fishing.* Add more related information to model elaboration. *The kids are fishing. They have already caught three fish. They brought a big bucket with them. I think they will put the fish in it.*

Read the text back as you write. End with a conspicuous period and make a clucking sound with your tongue. If someone asks why you did that, tell the class you do that to remember to put a period. Have children read the paragraph with you and ask them if you hit the target.

Kindergarten Modeled Writing

In kindergarten, some of your modeled writing will be adult writing. Other times, be sure to model for each level of your emergent writers: writing with strings of random letters, strings of the letters of your name, starting consonants with a letter-to-word correspondence and finger spaces, starting and end consonants with a word correspondence, using transitional spelling with dashes for the unidentified missing letters. Seeing these models empowers children to write, even though they cannot do it in an adult fashion. If all your modeling is in adult writing, children will say, "I can't do that," and they will give up.

Step 4: Students Try It Out

Begin the writing component of your workshop by telling your young writers to write anything they want about their picture, but to aim for the target—"Remember what you told your partner about the picture yesterday." Some children will ask if they can have a knee-to-knee conference to talk about the picture again. Good idea. Some children will ask if they should draw a target and put an H in the corner of the paper. Those who ask should do it. When other writers see that, many of them will copy the idea.

Close the writing workshop with an Author's Chair or peer sharing before students put their writing away.

Lauren   Practice
    Key Words:
Pounce sitting staring lines
Speckeled gripping smiling Surrounded

    In this picture I see a frog and he is smiling. This frog is sitting on a dark rock that looks like it has gold on it. The frog is staring at you in the picture and looks as if it were going to pounce on top of an animal or fish. Also, It looks as if it were gripping the rock for some strage redson.

Grade 4 Target Skill Writing.

Model the Picture-Prompted Writing Process Again and Again

As with all your models, you should repeat this one from time to time, focusing on a different Target Skill each time. Always do each exercise both orally and in writing. Start with a simple descriptive skill and move on to include the skills detailed in the rest of this book—the writing-craft techniques utilized by writers of creative nonfiction.

Display the current week's Target Skill(s) on a bulletin board reserved for writing, in a reserved space on your blackboard/whiteboard, and in writing centers.

Teachers who set up centers for independent work introduce a Target Skill on Monday and establish it as the target the children will use during the week in a writing center. They post Target Skills in the center. Even as early as the first and second grade, students often remember Target Skills from previous weeks and carry them forward to their new writing.

Chapter 2: **Organizing Informational Writing**

Expository writers, denied the linear chronological order that guides story writers, must find other logical and natural ways to present information or explain things. They must help their readers deal with many facts and ideas, make sense of them, and remember them. Here are some of the organizing techniques they employ:

- moving from the general to specific
- using natural divisions within a topic
- following a logical order based on place or time
- presenting a sequence of steps in a process
- comparing two people, places, or things

Helping Readers Remember

Readers remember information more easily if it is presented in an organized fashion. When we organize bits of seemingly random information we give them meaning.

Try this experiment with your students:
- Select three words from three categories, such as fruit, furniture, and musical instruments. Example: chair, orange, table, drum, banana, trumpet, lamp, violin, apple. (In first grade, use just six words and select two words from each of the three categories.)
- List the nine words in random order and spacing on the board.
- Read the list twice with the children.
- Ask two volunteers to step outside the classroom and wait to be called back in.

- While the volunteers are gone, quickly put up a prepared chart with the nine words listed in three named groups: Fruit: orange, banana, apple; Furniture: chair, table, lamp; Musical Instruments: drum, trumpet, violin.

Fruit	Furniture	Musical Instruments
orange	chair	drum
banana	table	trumpet
apple	lamp	violin

- Read the list twice with the children.
- Send two more volunteers out into the hall.
- Remove the lists of words.
- Call the first two children back in and ask each, one after the other, to tell quickly what words he or she remembers of the nine. Write their words on two pieces of paper and give them to a student secretary.
- Now call the second two children in, the ones who read and heard the words clumped into three categories. Ask them, one after the other, to tell quickly what words they remember. Write their lists of words on separate papers. Have the secretary read the lists of words the first volunteers remembered. Read the second volunteers' lists and ask the class to compare them with the earlier lists.

Invariably, the children who hear, read, and say the list when the items are clumped in the three categories remember more of the words. Why? Because it is easier to remember organized information than random information.

Keep referring to this activity as you teach your students about organizing their informational writing. Remind them—"Think of your reader, who is trying to remember and understand your information."

Young Writers' Schemes for Informational Writing

The following schemes for organizing informational writing (writing that deals with concrete facts) are useful to young developing writers in first grade and higher. Emergent writers in kindergarten and first grade are not ready to organize their writing—they just jump right in. Every day is a new adventure in writing. They do, however, respond to Target Skill lessons, particularly composing skills (see Chapter 3). And, they can take part in the oral and shared writing components of the following lessons about organization.

- general-to-specific example: Describe an urban setting in general, then describe a variety of cities in the United States.
- natural divisions within a topic example: Baseball: rules, players, equipment, field
- divisions based on place or time example: Layers of the rain forest, or a northern forest in fall, winter, spring, and summer
- steps in a process example: How to make ice cream

Books as Models

Lists of Capstone nonfiction texts that illustrate the various organizational schemes described here are presented in the following pages at the start of each lesson, specific to the scheme.

General to specific: The main idea is revealed in the first page and the remainder of the book is devoted to specific examples of the idea.

Natural divisions: Related information is presented in clumps. The book's table of contents reveals how the author divided the information.

Divisions based on time: Information is presented in season sequence.

Divisions based on place: Information is arranged in a sequence of places or parts making up the whole.

Steps in a process: Information is presented as a series of steps that explain how to do something, or to describe a process or a cycle.

Critical-thinking Skills

The mental processes we must go through to organize our expository writing are what we commonly refer to as critical thinking skills. Every education improvement plan includes the teaching of such skills as a prominent objective. Writing instruction is an excellent vehicle for achieving that objective. Every expository writer discovers that writing is thinking—we can't write coherently about a topic we haven't thought about and organized. And, at the same time, the very act of writing helps us develop our thoughts and refine our organization.

Sorting and classifying, comparing, creating analogies, understanding similes and metaphors, and seeing patterns, sequences, and other logical relationships between objects, people, events, and ideas—these are all critical thinking skills. They are also critical organizing and composing skills for writers. Thus, good writing instruction teaches young students critical thinking skills and how to apply them to communicate effectively. Whether students do any writing after they leave school, they need these skills to succeed in their jobs and in their lives.

Lessons

A. General-to-Specific Scheme (grades K–4)

Animal Migration

Big, Bigger, Biggest

Bread Around the World

Everybody Moves

Getting There

Leading the Way

Our Five Senses

Parks of the U.S.A.

Save the Animals

Science Measurements

The Bill of Rights

Weather Watchers: Weather (SRT)

Introduce the Concept (Awareness) (grades K–4)

Read to your students one of the mentor texts you selected. Ask students to predict what the book is about after you have read the title and the first page. Now point out how the author, after telling what the book is about in general, uses the rest of the book to give many specific examples.

Example: *Animal Migration*

The entire book is about the general topic of animal migration. Each section is about a specific animal that migrates.

Finish reading the book together. Count the number of examples. How many pages are devoted to each example? Compare the information from page to page.

More Examples

Read other informational books that use a general-to-specific organization. Discuss and review the organization with your students. Ask older students to find examples in their independent reading and report them to the class.

Try It Out Orally (grades K–4)

You can help young children understand the general-to-specific concept by playing the **Categories** game with them.

Categories Game

Prepare a list of some general topics and a list of some of the specifics. (I have started a list of general topics for you. You can add others that relate to topics your class is studying. Fill in the specific examples.)

General	Specific
Games we play	Hide and Seek, Nintendo, stick ball, kickball, ...
Trees	apple, pine, oak, maple, orange, ...
Trucks	mail, dump, pick-up, concrete, fire, ...
Cereals	Cheerios, Rice Krispies, oatmeal, ...
Houses	
Sports	
Birds	
Famous leaders	
Presidents' states	
Farm animals	
Our class activities or centers	
Habitats	
Planets	
Bears	

Explain the game to the children with several examples. "If I say cereal, I want you to give me a specific example of a cereal, such as Cheerios. If I say flower, I would like you to tell me a specific flower, such as rose or tulip." Play the game in its oral form several times in an informal round.

In **kindergarten,** show your class how to make **Fist Lists.** Raise your hand in a fist. That is the topic. Now unfold each finger as you give a specific example of the general category. Fist: toys. Fingers: matchbox car, squeaky duck, doll, truck. Have kids use both hands as the list grows.

In **higher grades,** conduct the game with a physical activity as well. Start with students sitting. When they say a specific example of the general term, they stand. If they give an incorrect answer, they just remain sitting. Always use this positive approach: rewarding a correct answer (stand up) instead of a negative approach: penalizing an incorrect answer (sit down).

Practice Variations of General to Specific

In writing centers, in morning tasks, during transitions, standing in line, whenever possible, play General-to-Specific Games and the reverse.

- Present a list of specifics and have kids identify the general category: spaghetti, macaroni, ziti, lasagna noodles, penne. All pasta.

- Present a list of specifics with a non-example thrown in: spaghetti, macaroni, rice, ziti, penne, lasagna. All pasta except rice.

Try It Out in Writing (grades K–4)

Have your students select a general topic from the game list or think up one of their own. Ask them to write a list of all the examples they can think of. They might work alone or in pairs. Share the lists in groups or as a whole class activity. Kindergarten students can make their lists by drawing, pasting pictures, or with you acting as the scribe in a shared writing activity.

Practice

At every opportunity, elementary students should make lists. The ability to categorize information is a critical thinking skill.

A First-Grade Example

From: *Michelle, Dunbar Magnet School, Tampa, FL.* After discussing and playing with the General-to-Specific concept with my first graders, I asked them to close their eyes and imagine they were in a car. *"Put on your seat belt, put the window down, here we go. You are at a stoplight. What do you see?"* I asked them to be specific; not a store but Publix, not a restaurant but McDonald's. After the children named one specific place they each could see, I gave them an index card and they drew the specific place and labeled it. Then I glued each place on a large sheet of butcher paper and the children drew streets, trees, buildings; creating a map of specific places.

1. Personal Expertise Lists (grades 1–4)

At the start of the school year, help your students develop a list of personal expertise topics. In all successful writing programs, children and adults learn the writing craft by writing about personal topics before they are asked to write to assignments and prompts. When we write about ourselves, we are engaged. We have control over the information and find it easier to elaborate on a topic we know well. A personal information piece is the perfect vehicle upon which to try out new writing skills.

Help the students place their personal topic items in categories:
- things they know
- places they have been
- people they know
- things they can do

Ask them to share their lists with other students in the class.

Kindergarten and first graders often make these lists by pasting magazine pictures that represent what they know, have experienced, etc., on a long strip of heavy paper. Some teachers ask parents to help students make this list as a homework activity. Second graders and older should keep these lists of potential writing topics in their writing journals or notebooks.

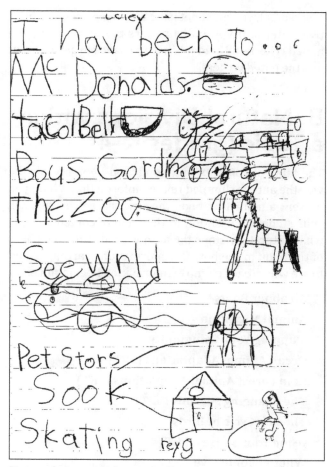

I hav been To...
Mc Donalds.
Tacol Bell
Boys Gordin.
The Zoo,
See Wrld
Pet Stors
Sook
Skating

First grader's personal expertise list.

2. Published Lists

Publish a classroom chart or class book of General-to-Specific lists. Each child contributes an item or a page with an accompanying drawing or picture. Invite the children to make a collection of these lists on their own.

Application

- Have your kindergarten through fourth-grade students publish general-to-specific lists on their own.

- Following an appropriate class thematic unit, assign second, third, and fourth graders an information piece using **general-to-specific** organization. The unit should be presented through activities, field trips, reading in both nonfiction and fiction, or art-related projects, i.e., immersion. During the thematic unit, have students keep a list of specific people, animals, plants, places, etc., representative of the topic.

Examples of thematic units that lend themselves to writing, using this organization scheme:

zoo animals: camel, tiger, lion, panda, polar bear, monkey, ...

community workers: mail deliverer, traffic officer, firefighter, ambulance driver, ...

mammals: cow, fox, bear, beaver, squirrel, kangaroo, possum, ...

birds: _____

insects: _____

trees: _____

endangered species: _____

U.S. rivers: _____

habitats: _____

Native Americans: _____

simple machines: _____

Thursday, Sept. 30:
Complete the chart below with your child by having a General/Specific Hunt in your house. Each general item should have at least three specific examples. You can write the words for your child, have your child draw pictures or have your child use beginning sounds and you complete the word.

General	Specific
Ice-Cream GP	Rainbows Pops Mini Ice-Cream Sandwiches Push-Ups
Kool-Aid	GRape TRopical PuNch Le MonADe
Chips	PRingles FuNyuns DORiTos

Parent and child general-to-specific homework.

First-Grade Example

Mary Beth's first graders at *Dunbar Magnet School in Tampa, FL,* worked on the general-to-specific concept over several days. They played Fist Lists and they built a class General and Specific chart. One of their general categories was *Movement.* They read a science Shared Reading Text about squirrels and noted all the specific movement words: *balance, leap, eat, hide,* etc. Then they each drew a movement on an index card and pasted them in the "Specific" column for *Movement* on the class chart.

Next, Mary Beth read *Play All Day* by Julie Paschkis, a book about a child who takes his reader through his day, sharing the different ways he plays: riding a horse, chasing a ball, reading, imaginary play, etc. During shared writing, the class listed all the ways they play. Then they each illustrated their list item on an index card and pasted it in the "Specific" column for *Play* on their General and Specific class chart. Later, they categorized, dividing the *Play* list into *Indoor Play* and *Outdoor Play.*

Kindergarten Example

Luana's kindergarten class at *Dunbar Magnet School* worked on the general-to-specific concept as well. They played General-to-Specific Fist List games, often during transition times during the day (a few minutes here and there when students are moving from one activity to another). They named specific shapes, colors, days, months, stores, animals, farm animals. "You name it, we probably did it," Luana reports. The class read a Shared Reading Text about apples and learned there are many different kinds of apples and ways to cook and eat them. During that week, Luana sent a general-to-specific assignment home for parents to help their children with the concept. See illustration on page 25.

Assessment

Criterion: Do the lists or the written piece demonstrate the general-to-specific concept?

Whenever you assess student writing, be sure to establish the Target Skill criteria for the piece. Be sure students know what they are. When you make your assessment, you must not use other, unspecified, subjective criteria. If you judge papers based on predetermined criteria, all students have a chance to get an A, not just the gifted writers.

B. Natural Divisions within a Topic (grades K–4)

The table of contents in a nonfiction book reveals the way the author clumped related information. When you present a nonfiction book through shared reading, call your students' attention to the table of contents to see what natural divisions the author used. Turn the pages of the book to see how the information is arranged and to see where each clump of information begins and ends.

All about Boats

Animal Migration

Mapping Your Community

Ocean Animal Adaptations (SRT)

Rain Forest Animal Adaptations (SRT)

The Changing Seasons (SRT)

The Life Cycle of Birds

Using Your Senses (SRT)

Where People Live

Introduce the Concept (Awareness) (grades K–4)

Share with your young writers one of the Capstone informational mentor texts that illustrates organization based on natural divisions—that is, clumps of related information within a topic. Ask them what they think the book is about after they have read the title. Show them how authors help their readers by telling them about the clumps of related information in the table of contents.

Example: *Ocean Animal Adaptations.* This book describes the adaptations ocean animals have made to survive. Each section tells about the different ways these animals move, hide, or catch food.

Notice that the author does not number the divisions of the topic as if there were an implied order of importance. Young writers should not be encouraged to start informational paragraphs with order orienters, such as First, Second, and Third. They should do this in describing a process where the order of the process steps is crucial or sometimes in persuasive pieces where writers conventionally present their arguments in order of importance or logic.

For example, in *Ocean Animal Adaptations,* an informational text, there is no hierarchy of importance of the adaptations, while in *Oranges: From Fruit to Juice,* a process-description text, sequence is important and the author uses words, such as during, when, first, after that, and the next step to alert the reader. See page 37, Steps in a Process.

More Examples

Gather more informational books, appropriate for your grade level. Choose those that have simple tables of contents. Ask your school librarian for other examples. As an informal class project, have children look through the books and tables of contents and take turns sharing, in whole class or reading groups, the book topics and the natural divisions or clumps the authors used.

Extend this activity to teach students that reading nonfiction is not like reading a story. You do not always need to read a nonfiction book from the start to finish as you do a story. You can skip around. You can start with different parts of the book—table of contents, pictures or graphics and their accompanying captions, the glossary, the index.

Practice (grades K–4)

Creating the natural divisions of a topic is an abstract thinking skill. Students in the concrete-operational stages, kindergarten to fourth grade, cannot do this in their heads. They can, however, do it through the concrete operation of **sorting.** That is, they can randomly list words or bits of information associated with a topic, then physically sort the bits into piles of related information.

Modeling Sorting

Model sorting for all your students. For example, your model using buttons might sound like this:

Some of the buttons have just two holes. They go together. Some of them have four holes, and they go together. And these have little loops on the back. They all go in a new pile. Or I could put all the plastic ones in one pile and all the metal ones in another.

Note that you *give a reason* for each division as you sort. When your students sort, be sure they articulate why they formed each group or clump.

Give your students compartmentalized, urethane food trays and have them sort objects: buttons, stones, seashells, zippers, seeds, small toys, pasta. Ask them to **explain their sorting schemes**. Physical sorting, clumping of objects, is a precursor skill to paragraphing, clumping of information.

Sorting

Sorting or grouping of items based on making comparisons is a critical thinking skill and an important science skill as well as a writing skill. Provide the opportunity for your elementary students to sort often. To build physical collections or charts of a sorting exercise, mark large pieces of chart paper or wrapping paper with wide rows and columns to form a grid of boxes (also called cells). These should be large enough for the youngest students to draw, paste pictures, or put objects in as they sort the pictures or objects into categories. A flat gift box, divided into small compartments by crosspieces of cardboard, or inserting small boxes within the larger one, creates a physical sorting table for small items. Help young children name the attributes and label each column. For example, if the box or chart is used to sort pasta, the attribute columns might be labeled: *curly, straight, hollow, flat, round.*

Try It Out in Writing (grades mid-first to 4)

After practicing sorting objects and symbols, and after seeing how writers of informational text sort and arrange information, young writers will be ready to organize their own written information, using a concrete sorting approach. You need to model how writers sort and clump the information they want to present to their readers. Here is a series of models that progresses from concrete to more abstract. You can use the first model with the youngest students. You should do the entire sequence for your second, third, and fourth graders. In grades three and four you also can show your young writers how this operation relates to the graphic organizer called a web.

A. First Model: Sorting Single-Word Cards (grades mid-first to 4)

Consider this a writing lesson, a science activity, and critical thinking development. It is all these things.

You will need:

- 12–15 pieces of 5" x 2" paper or card stock, for each student. (One of the best sources for this paper is a print shop where personnel will save scraps at your request.)
- 12–15 large index cards with a small magnet or piece of mounting putty on the back of each.

Procedure:

Review the Capstone book you chose to introduce this lesson. Remind your young writers that related information—the things that go together in clumps—are placed close together in the book. Tell your students that you are planning to write your own informational book about places you go. Make a random list of places, one place to each index card, and think aloud as you make the list. You can also do this on an overhead projector with pieces of transparencies cut into 2" x 3" rectangles. Place a few of the cards on the board as you work. (Over the course of the exercise, you will add several more to the board until you display 12–15 cards.)

When you have several *place* cards on the board, stop and invite your students to each make a similar list, one place per card or slip of paper. (Have children put their initials on the back of each card.) Rove and encourage them to help one another with writing the words. Do not place an emphasis on spelling or the task will take too long. (In your model pretend you do not know how to write a word, sound it out but write it incorrectly, and circle it. Tell your students you will find out later how to spell it.)

Encourage students to talk quietly as they work and to share place words. Talk with students to help them complete their lists. This listing activity can be extended through the day, into homework, and the model continued on the following day. Give your students rubber bands or envelopes in which to keep their word cards.

When children have 12–15 places listed, gather the class to consider your cards, displayed on the board or projected the screen. Ask your students if they see which cards belong together. Call on several volunteers, in turn, to come to the board and physically sort your cards into clumps of related places. Have students

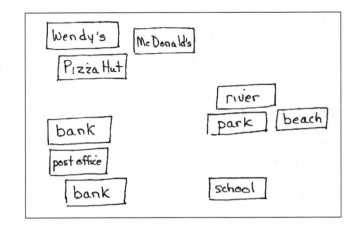

articulate the reason places belong together. *McDonald's should go with Wendy's and Pizza Hut, they are all restaurants. You can put the park with the beach and the river, they are all outside places. The post office and bank belong with the library, they are all buildings you go to when you are not here, Mrs. Freeman.*

Add extra cards to label each group. For example: *Places I Go to Eat, Places I Play, Places I Go Outside.*

Now invite students to sort **their** places into related clumps. Give them more blank papers if they ask. Have students read their cards to a partner and tell what each of their clumps is about. Have them write a label card, the rationale, for each of their groups.

When they have completed the sorting task, bring their attention back to your model. Tell them you have to make a decision about which clump should go first. Choose a clump and number each card in that clump with a "1." Choose another and label those cards "2," and so forth. Ask your students to decide which of their clumps they will put first, second, etc.

Next, write the title of your piece on a new index card or piece of transparency: *Places I Like to Go* or *Places I Go.* Ask students to do the same. When they are ready, ask them to place all the clumps in order: Title, clump 1 label card and the cards in the group, clump 2 label card and the cards in the group, etc. Walk through the class and staple their papers along the left-hand side to form little booklets. As you complete them, invite student partners to read their books to each other by telling about each place in their little Shared Reading Text.

The stapled booklet, which they may choose to illustrate, is the finished product. Do this exercise many times in a school year. After ample practice, in grades two and above, do the exercise using half sheets of paper instead of the cards. When your young writers list words, have them put each word at the top or corner of the page. Now there is room on the pages for students to write several sentences about each word and to illustrate the information on the opposite pages. Work on this booklet may be extended over several months with students adding new information, revising their text to new Target Skills and editing for capitalization, punctuation, and spelling. The finished product may be used as the dummy for a hand-published or computer-published version at the end of the project.

Pages of a second grader's organized information booklet.

B. Second Model: Sorting Sentence Strips (grades 1–4)

You will need:

- 10–12 strips of card stock, 3" by 16". On each, write brief sentences of information about a universal topic, such as "dogs." (Dogs are carnivores. Dogs growl. They bite. Dogs have tails. They have whiskers. Dogs pant. Dogs eat bones. Dogs eat Puppy Chow, etc. Include one that does not relate to any of the others, a non sequitur, such as: My grandfather has a big hound dog.)

- a large sheet of blank newsprint or printed newspaper
- glue sticks, paste, or masking tape

Procedure:

Gather your class at the easel (primary grades). Call your older students for a writing lesson in the fashion you prefer. Display an informational Shared Reading Text or a regular-sized book that you've previously used to show how an author groups information that goes together.

> **All about Boats:** early boats, working boats, fun boats, boats in the future
>
> **Ocean Animal Adaptations:** ocean animal body parts, body coverings, behavior

Remind your young writers that related information—the things that go together in clumps—are placed close together in the book. Show them a few pages to help them recall.

Next, have them read the card strips about dogs and place them in an open space on the floor. Ask your students to sort them into groups of sentences that go together. Help them find and articulate the *reasons* why some belong together. When they try to deal with the unrelated one, tell them they can toss it away once they see it doesn't belong in any of the clumps. Explain to students that writers don't use everything they know about a topic in one article.

When the sorting is complete, ask the children which clump they would like to have first, next, next, ..., last. Move the clumps to the positions they chose.

Next, ask them to put the sentences within each clump in the order they think is best. Often a discussion will arise concerning the logic of sentence position. A child might think **Dogs growl** should go before **Dogs bite**. *That's what the dog does just before it bites, so it should go first.* Great, your young writers are beginning to see that writing requires thinking. Moving the sentence strips around illustrates an important revision principle: You can move text.

Paste or tape the strips in groups on the large sheet of paper, leaving some space between groups and leaving some room at the top for a title. Hang the large piece of paper, and have your young writers read the resulting text. They may suggest a title.

The finished product is a paste-up. The writing will not be graceful and it may not flow logically. There is no beginning or ending. There is no mention of indentation. No matter. You are concerned here only with having the children understand the clumping (paragraphing) principle. You will find lessons about beginnings, endings, and transitions later in this book. But first things first: There can be no effective beginning, ending, or transitions in a piece that is not logically organized.

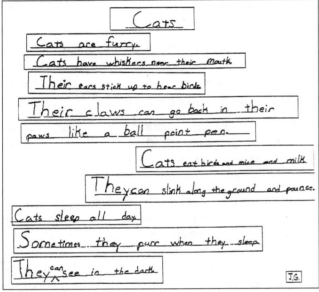

Second grader sorts information strips to organize her writing.

3. Third Model: List Linking (grades 2–4)

Until young writers can abstractly divide a topic into its important or natural aspects or develop a corresponding abstract graphic planner, such as a web, lists serve as a wonderful prewriting tool. When your students are facile with listing and physical sorting as demonstrated in the first two models, you can move to a more abstract organizing tool, which I call **list linking**.

Model a list of random words about a topic for your students.

Then, have them do the same with a topic they choose for themselves—something they know about. (Refer them to their start-of-the-year personal expertise lists.) They can make their lists as you build yours. Do not ask them to make their lists on a regular 8" x 11" sheet of paper. Have them fold it lengthwise or provide them with long strips of paper for this activity.

Next, show them how you connect items on your list that go together using pencil lines.

This is called **list linking**. Invite them to do the same. When they are ready, have each child name his or her topic and tell what items he or she linked and why. The articulation of why items go together is essentially the topic sentence, graceless though it may be. For example, in this topic list about fishing, the student might say: *This clump is about what fish I catch. This paragraph is about what equipment I use. This paragraph is about where I go fishing.*

As in the previous models, have young writers select and number the clumps or paragraphs they want to place first, second, third, fourth, etc.

Have your students practice **list linking** often without writing afterward about their topics. List linking is an excellent prewriting tool for them to use on a prompted, expository writing assessment. It, and physical sorting, are the concrete-operational precursors to the abstract task of webbing.

Provide many opportunities for your students to use this method of organizing their informational writing. Use the technique during a thematic unit. Some examples of thematic units that lend themselves to the organization scheme of clumping information into its natural divisions are:

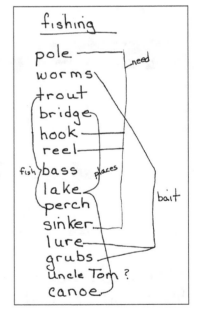

- Antarctic habitat
- desert habitat
- five senses
- food
- growing plants
- human body
- jobs
- money
- Native American tribes
- water
- weather

Lauren   Practice

                              list linking ←

Justin Timberlake
◊ N'sync
○ Basketball
□ Tennessee
□ blue eyes
◊ pop music
◊ costumes
□ curly
□ Curly, Bounce
△ Here we go
△ Tearin' up my Heart
△ Merry Christmas, Happy Holidays
□ 18 years old
○ Shaq O'neal
□ He doesn't like his curly hair
△ Cd
◊ concert, Orlando

A fourth grader uses a code to clump related items.

From Sorting and Classifying to Webbing (grades 3–4)

Show your third and fourth graders the relationship between the physical sorting of information they have done and the creation of a graphic organizer called a web. Show them that the clumps they created are the subtopic portions of a web. The items in their clumps are the details that are added to the web. They have just built one backward—gathering the details first, then naming the clump. Demonstrate this relationship, but do not require that these students create a web as prewriting until they can do it independently.

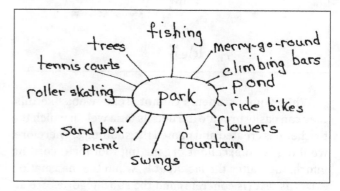

Fourth grader numbers the order of clumps (paragraphs).

A Special Note about Webbing

Webbing is NOT a useful prewriting graphic planner for young elementary school student writers because it requires them to gather, hold, sort, and classify facts and ideas in their heads. That is an abstract task and as Piaget pointed out, early elementary student ages 5 to around 10 are in the concrete-operational stages of mental development. (Please refer here to your Educational Psychology course notes.)

When we ask young children to create webs, they look like this.

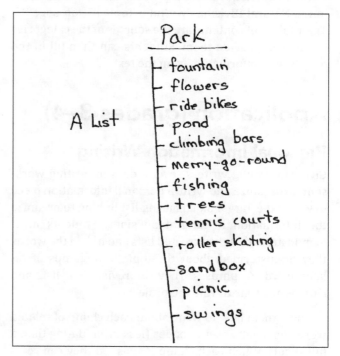

Break the circle anywhere and stretch the line vertically. You will find that this is a list drawn in circular form. Young writers are great at making lists.

The following diagram *is* a true web. It required us to create the subtopics or divisions of the main idea in our head.

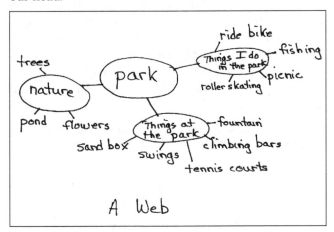

A Web

While young students cannot create webs like this, they can easily provide the details for a web in which the teacher has created and named the subtopics. Therefore, webbing is an excellent organizing tool for recording information after the fact; that is, when the information exists as text (is concrete) and the subcategories are already established.

You and your students can build webs as a shared writing experience using any of the mentor texts listed in the Natural Divisions within a Topic list on page 26. Their tables of contents are the sources of the categories or you can provide them. Students can then fill in the details with information from the text.

Application (grades 3–4)

Personal Information Writing

Give your young writers several days in writing workshop to organize and write a personal information piece in which the Target Skill is using list linking to organize the information in natural divisions. Students must demonstrate that they created lists and linked the words they brainstormed about the topic into clumps of related words or phrases. They can revise their lists and clumps any time during the project.

Show them how to write about each clump of related words on a half sheet of paper (less intimidating than a full sheet). When each clump is finished they can rearrange the half sheets (paragraphs) in an order they feel is appropriate having seen the written information in its entirety.

Follow these organization lessons with ones about beginnings and endings. (See Chapter 4.) Young writers can add beginnings and endings to their pasted information practice pieces as a revision task. Model how to do this by adding a beginning and an ending to the saved demonstration piece about dogs. (See page 29.)

Revising a Writing Plan
Always allow writers to modify their prewriting plan and their writing as they go. This may not be the model we remember from high school, where we had to turn in an outline before we wrote a piece (and woe to us if we didn't follow the outline). We got around that stricture by writing the piece first, then making the outline and handing it in, and finally tidying up the written piece to follow. What writers so often find is that as they write, i.e., *think*, they see a new and better direction to go or a different focus to take. Forcing a writer to stick to his first plan is folly and counterproductive.

Professional writers often write the beginning of an information article after the middle or body of the piece is complete. At that point, they know where they have taken their readers and can create an appropriate hook and introduction that will engage their readers and lead them into the piece.

Assessment

When you evaluate a student's first or early application of an organizing scheme, evaluate the piece only for that single Target Skill. This will encourage the young writer. If you find a dozen other things he has done wrong in the piece, do not penalize him, but do use this information to diagnose instructional needs.

Older students can handle 2–4 Target Skills in an independent piece when they have had ample demonstration, practice, and success with single a Target Skill application. (See other Target Skills in the area of composing and conventions in subsequent chapters of this book.)

C. Divisions Based on Time (grades K–4)

A Bee's Life (SRT)

Desert Seasons

Fossils

From Egg to Snake

If the Shoe Fits

To Fly in the Sky

Who Reached the South Pole First?

Introduce the Concept (Awareness) (grades K–4)

Using one of the suggested titles or any book that you have that is organized based on time, show students the contents and point out the different "time" elements (such as seasons or months of the year). Now read the text slowly and ask students to tell you when they hear the information change from one time element to the next. Have them reiterate the different time divisions in order, if that is applicable.

Practice (grades K–4)

The Concept of Seasons

In some regions of the country the change of seasons is a difficult concept for primary students. In southern Florida, for example, the change of seasons is visually subtle compared to northern states where fall color displays dazzle and winter snows glisten. Teachers in Florida have to make do with hurricane, citrus, fishing, football, baseball, and tourist seasons. The study of climatic seasons becomes a vicarious experience, with photographs providing most of the information. (See Chapter 5 for the role of pictures in informational writing.)

Invite your students to collect magazine pictures of activities in the different seasons. Use the pictures to make class lists and charts that show seasonal differences. Examples: Winter Games/Summer Games; Trees in Winter, Spring, Summer, and Fall; Seasonal Sports; Winter Clothes—Summer Clothes; Four Seasons On the Farm, In the City, In School.

Try It Out Orally (grades K–4)

Discuss other time periods besides the seasons.

- **A day:** Activities in the morning at home, on the way to school, at school, lunch hour, more classes, after school, evening.
- **A school day:** Getting there, morning-opening activities, writing workshop, music, math, lunch, physical education, science, computer lab.
- **Day and night:** Sunrise, eat, work, play, sunset, sleep.
- **The week:** Days of the week and special activities on certain days.
- **The year:** Months, holidays, and birthdays in each.

Try It Out in Writing (grades 1–4)

Invite students to show how they would divide their day into components. Show them how to use a storyboard, a pie chart, or a timeline (the latter two are more abstract than storyboard) to organize their information.

Ask your students to write an informational piece about their school day. Remind them that the Target Skill of the piece is to *organize their information into time segments.* Encourage them to create ways to show the divisions. The kindergartners' book, ***From Sun Up to Sun Down*** (see next two pages), used the position of the sun, on a construction paper sky, to show morning, afternoon, evening, and night.

D. Divisions Based on Place (grades K–4)

Animals with No Eyes

Look Inside a Tree

Monsters of the Deep

A Kindergarten Example

Luana's kindergarten students at Dunbar Magnet School, Tampa, FL, studied nonfiction Shared Reading Texts about the seasons of the year and squirrels lives through a year. They discussed the seasons in terms of their own knowledge. Some children had seen colorful leaves and snow in the North. Next, they made a pie chart collage of pictures of clothing divided into the four seasons. Then they discussed how a day was divided into different times and different activities. For homework, children made lists—written, dictated, or drawn—of their daily activities. When they gathered for writing workshop, they each contributed, in a shared writing, to a class list of what they do all day. Then they each illustrated their contribution to make a page for their class book, *From Sun Up to Sun Down.*

... update our calendar.

When the sun goes down we ...

... eat dinner.

Introduce the Concept (Awareness) (grades K–4)

Show your students the cross-section of a sandwich, a piece of layer cake, or a diagram showing geological layers. Talk about layers. Ask students if they can think of anything else that has layers. Answers might include: Oreo cookies, blankets and quilts on a bed, a house, layers of clothing in cold weather, etc. Chart their ideas.

Use a dollhouse to show the parts of a house, starting with the roof and moving downward. Children might mention a basement or cellar. Tell your young writers that authors often explain or describe something that has layers and, when they do, they do it in sequence to help their readers understand or picture that thing.

Models from Books

Read one of the listed mentor text titles that take a reader from layer to layer or from one place to another in order to reveal information about the whole in an organized fashion. Have students indicate when they see or hear an author begin a new layer or section.

Try It Out Orally (grades 1–4)

Help students find the words in the text indicating *place*. Make a list on chart paper as children identify them.

The following place indicators come from the mentor texts listed for this lesson:

> *on top, near, at the bottom, on the floor, upper, along, lower, out, the end, in the highest, at the top, around, from above, all over, where, top level, here, going down to, among, at this level, on the bottom level, up here, closest, third from the sun, over there, the last, back on, home*

Using photographs or photo cards, have your students, in pairs, tell each other about their pictures, focusing on giving the location of things and using some of the words from the chart. They might prompt each other with the question: *Where is the _____?* Model this conference for your students with an articulate student.

Trying It Out in Writing (grades 1–4)

After the prewriting conferences, have students write briefly to tell about their pictures, with *using location words* as the Target Skill.

Organizing a piece (grades 3–4)

Take your students on a walking tour of the schoolyard to explore the places that make up the whole. If they carry clipboards they can note features and nearby landmarks. *(The baseball backstop is near the big hedge around the schoolyard. The front entrance has a flag on the side. The bike rack is near the Media Center door.)* Students might construct maps of the area as an additional activity.

Upon returning to the classroom, ask students to share their information. On a large paper, draw the outline of the schoolyard. Ask students, in groups, to decide on the plan for the order of their descriptive statements: from the front to back, from the building out to the boundaries of the yard, from the boundaries in toward the building, from one side to the other, from the center outward. Have the groups of students pool their information and write about the schoolyard, using the plan they formulated.

Invite students to write about topics from the layered-places list they created during the Awareness component of this lesson or any other they choose that can be described in terms of places or parts that make up the whole. Remind them to organize the piece by selecting a sequence in which to describe the layers or parts of the place or thing.

Ask them to draw pictures, diagrams, or maps to help their readers visualize the layers or places. They might write about a dollhouse, the schoolyard, their street, the classroom, or layers of clothing on a cold day. Or they may choose to describe something from top to bottom, such as a tree, a house, an apartment building, a farm, a scarecrow, or one wall of the classroom. Their objective is to organize the piece by moving the reader from place to place, helping their reader by using *where* words.

Group Assignments

Assign jobs for group activities: recorder, illustrator, scout (roams to see what other groups are doing and brings back ideas), and reporter. These four jobs accommodate and encompass the different learning styles children use, as well as the language arts components: speaking, listening, visual interpretation, writing, and reading.

Ocean Floor IN PROGRESS 11-2-95

"If you were diving on the continental shelf you would see lots of fish and plants, because there is a lot of sunlight on the continental shelf.

If you kept on diving you would see the continental slope. The canyons on the continental slope could be deeper than the Grand Canyon. They can be two miles long or more.

Fourth grader uses a diver as a transitional device to show layers of ocean floor.

E. Steps in a Process (grades K–4)

Cooking Pancakes

Making Maple Syrup

Oranges: From Fruit to Juice

You Can Write an Amazing Journal

Introduce the Concept (Awareness) (grades K–4)

Introduce process description following an art, craft, or science activity during which your students performed a sequence of steps to make a product. Entertain your students with a very jumbled account of how to make the thing they just completed. They will stop you and tell you what you did wrong.

Discuss with your students why it matters that you tell how to do it in the correct order. Have some of them describe how they made their product.

In a shared writing session, write the steps on separate strips of paper, then have your students verify the order and arrange the strips accordingly. (Students can consult any sets of directions they were given at the start of their project.) Fasten the strips to the board or a chart.

Models from Books (grades K–4)

Read several mentor texts that describe processes. Do this over the course of several days in writing workshop. If you have sets of photo cards from process-description mentor texts, invite primary students to arrange the photos in order. The blackboard or whiteboard tray is a good place to arrange the cards in sequence.

Help the children find the transition words that authors use to guide the reader. List them on a chart. They will include: *start, first, begins, next, slowly, after some time, in a few hours, now, then, now it's time, before, as, soon, until, in the fall, in the summer, every spring, meanwhile, it's time, etc.*

Try It Out Orally (grades 1–4)

Describe a process to your students. Examples: how you wash your dog, how to set up a tent, how to do laundry, how you calculate their report card grades. Use as many step transition words as you can. Ask for volunteers to describe a process they do: a chore, how to add a column of single-digit numbers, how to take care of the class gerbil, how to get from one place to another.

Demonstrate the use of imperative verb tense when writing steps in a process or directions: Turn right at the office. Walk straight down the hall. Knock on the first door.

Try It Out in Writing (grades 2–4)

- Make a class chart of processes that occur in the students' daily lives: making a bed, getting to school, making a snack, shopping for shoes, sending an e-mail.
- Walk your class from your room to the cafeteria, media center, or gym. Carry a clipboard with 6–8 sentence strips. When you get to a place where you have to make a decision, stop and ask your class what to do. Write the direction they agree upon on one of the strips. Number the strips successively. Hold each one up for everyone to repeat/read. Continue to your destination.

When you return to class, in a shared writing session, write the directions to the destination on chart paper, using the sentence strips to guide the class. Invite a parent to class and have the class take him or her to the destination using the directions. (The parent can read the appropriate direction step aloud as the class reaches each decision point.) Older students can draw maps using the printed directions.

- Divide your class into groups of three. Ask one child to be the recorder and one to be the illustrator. Have the third student perform a five-step process, such as making a cracker and peanut butter sandwich or folding a paper airplane. Ask each group to help its recorder and illustrator write and draw what the third student does at each step of the process. Then have each child write a description of the process. Make a transition word list available to them: *first, next, after that, when, then, before, etc.*

For more about processes, see Flow Diagrams in Presenting Information Graphically, Chapter 5.

Practice and Application

Provide opportunities to practice writing descriptions of processes and directions. Establish this organization scheme with its attendant *vocabulary of order* (transition words) as a Target Skill for independent writing. Integrate map work, directions; physical education, how to play games or sports; art, how-to directions; science, procedure directions; math, algorithm descriptions, with the teaching and practice of this genre form.

Chapter 3: **Composing Skills**

Composing skills are all the wonderful means authors use to write in a clear, lively, graceful, and engaging manner. We call those aggregate skills the writing craft.

Writers of all ages can learn the craft. Primary students, just learning to write, are becoming aware of the control they have over their message. They are ready to be introduced to basic craft skills, many of which they can master by the end of fourth and fifth grade.

In this chapter you will learn how to use nonfiction mentor texts as a source of writing-craft models for both primary children and older elementary students. Older students love the big, photo-illustrated books they remember from their primary grade experience and they like to use them again in new ways. They are usually able to read the text independently and focus on the writing craft the authors demonstrate.

You should continue to point out craft skills to your students as you read other nonfiction texts to them. Make classroom charts listing examples of the skills that students find in their independent reading. (Always write the children's initials after their contributions to such lists.) Publish these charts for second, third, and fourth graders to keep in their writer's notebooks and to use as reference aids when they write.

Lessons

A. Description

Description, fundamental to all the genres, is a good place to start writing instruction. Descriptive writing instruction takes advantage of children's natural curiosity and observational prowess. Through our models and lessons, they learn how to use the vocabulary of description to express their observations.

Science/Writing Connect

Observation and description are fundamental to science as well as to writing. Many of the lessons in this chapter are important science activities. In the primary grades, the Common Core State Standards and the Next Generation Science Standards include *observation and description* benchmarks. Children are natural scientists at this age; they are discovering things about their surroundings— their environment. Provide time for them to observe, make discoveries, and talk about them. Encourage them to do so.

I advise starting the year's writing instruction program with picture-prompted descriptive writing. After you have shown your students how to use photographs in the Target Skill Concept lesson (see Chapter 1), have them use pictures for practice writing while they are learning the procedures of a daily writing workshop. Encourage them to use pictures that they draw as well.

As soon as you have introduced the target skill lesson, select *descriptive attributes* from the list on page 44 to serve as targets for your young writers' descriptions of photos and their own drawings. Introduce them, using the craft-lesson sequence described in the introduction of this book.

1. Describing with Verbs (grades K–4)

Verbs are the hallmark of good description. Readers want action, things happening, not static images. Teach your young writers to use verbs in description instead of relying heavily on adjectives: *The rabbit nibbles on carrots*, instead of *The rabbit has an orange carrot.* Or *Mike runs as fast as the wind*, instead of *Mike is fast.* When readers hear that the rabbit and Mike are **doing** something, they perceive the writing as being livelier—they can picture what's going on.

Focusing on what people, animals, and things are **doing**, also helps writers avoid sentences that start with the deadly *There is, There are,* and *It is,* or *He has, She has,* and *It has.* Good writers let their readers know what is going on. They write, *The temperature goes up during the day,* instead of *It gets hot.* They write, *The rabbit's white fur camouflages it in the snow,* instead of *The rabbit has white fur in the winter.*

Strong-verb writing is one of the most important craft skills you can teach. When children's writing vocabulary is still small, just focusing on verbs is a significant goal. As writers mature and their vocabularies grow, they can consider verb synonyms to find the very best descriptive verbs.

Capstone titles that illustrate strong-verb writing:

Animals with No Eyes

Coral Reefs: Colorful Underwater Habitats (SRT)

Countries Around the World: Brazil

Countries Around the World: Chile

Countries Around the World: Czech Republic

Flesh-Eating Machines

From Mealworm to Beetle (SRT)

Let's Rock: Metamorphic Rocks

Look Inside a Tree

Meat-Eating Plants and Other Extreme Plant Life

Ocean Animal Adaptations (SRT)

Polar Animal Adaptations (SRT)

Rain Forest Animal Adaptations (SRT)

The Story of Corn

Tundras

Which Seed Is This? (SRT)

Introduce the Concept (Awareness) (grades K–4)

Use covers of the mentor texts or photographs to show children how to use action words when they describe. Gather your class and talk about writing that really attracts readers. Remind your students about the difference between "Dinky Writing" and "Good Writing."

Show your class a mentor text cover or photograph and say sentences about the picture that are Dinky Writing and sentences that are Good Writing. (Yes, equate *talking* with *writing.*) Have students signal a *thumbs-up* and *thumbs-down* when they hear the two versions.

Your lesson might begin: *Listen to this, kids. I am going to show you two ways you can write about a picture. One way will be boring and one will be lively. They will be examples of Dinky Writing and Good Writing.*

Using a photograph or cover of a mentor text that shows children engaged in physical activity talk about the picture using Dinky Sentences, such as:

> *There are five kids. They are in an empty room. They have red, blue, and yellow shirts. They have sneakers on.*

Then say something like this:

> *Three kids are **exercising** or **dancing.** I don't know which. They are **bending** and **waving** their arms. I think they are **enjoying** the dancing.*

Ask your young writers which description they prefer; which is more fun to hear. Select a page of the mentor text and model some more Dinky Writing and Good (strong verb) Writing. (Students in one primary class I visit make "muscles" with their arms to signal when they hear Strong-Verb Writing.)

Models from Books (grades K–4)

- Read one of the listed mentor texts or a favorite shared reading book you have that is replete with fresh, active verbs. Point out the action words the author uses. In the mentor text, **The Story of Corn,** some verbs are: *peel, grind, figured out, popped, served, stored, sticking, sweeten, fix, unrolls, attached, harvest.* List the verbs identified in the shared reading on a class chart.

- The mentor text, **Polar Animal Adaptations,** provides a wealth of active verbs: *wear, tucks, trap, soaks, change, match, suffer, chop, snoozes, hibernates, migrate,* and *survive.* Tag this mentor text for future use for its illustration of comparisons, both simple and advanced, as well as a variety of supporting details—all writing-craft elements you will find described later in this book.

Try It Out Orally (grades K–3)

- In kindergarten and first grade, have the children, in a class group, practice saying Dinky Writing and Good Writing sentences about photo cards, mentor text covers, their own drawings, or pictures cut from magazines. Teach them to give a *thumbs-down* for Dinky Writing and a *thumbs-up* for Good Writing. This will encourage them to listen for and to recognize strong verbs that tell *what is happening*.

A Kindergarten Example

(From: *Luana, kindergarten, Dunbar Magnet School, Tampa, FL*) To begin a strong-verb word bank, we innovated on *Five Little Monkeys Jumping on the Bed*. We changed jumping to: rolling, spinning, twisting, running, flipping, sleeping, etc. Then we performed the new version as a class play with puppets. Now the children are using the verbs they find in our classroom library of animal books.

- Ask second, third, and fourth graders, *in peer partnerships,* to describe a picture they select from the classroom file or a family or school snapshot. Encourage them to base their description entirely upon *what is happening* (action) in the picture. Model one for your students first, such as:

Our class is <u>playing</u> ball in this photo. Tom is the one <u>pitching</u>. He always throws too low. We <u>yell</u> at him <u>to play</u> fair. Paula is <u>trying to steal</u> third. She <u>didn't make it</u>. Tom <u>tagged</u> her out.

- Build a verb chart on which students each paste an action picture cut from a magazine. Help them write the verb(s) portrayed in the picture. Remember to put the contributor's initials next to the entry. "That one's mine!" young writers will point out proudly.

- Build a class word bank of verbs illustrated with stick figures in action on a piece of poster board. Make it an ongoing project, with students adding more action words as they find them.

- In intermediate grades, have your students build their own stick-figure charts. One way to do this is have them draw the stick figures in dark marker over figures in magazine pictures. Enlist the help of the physical education and art teachers to demonstrate movement and body position in athletics and to help students draw moving figures. Have students build a list of synonyms for some of the verbs, using a Junior Thesaurus.

- **Verb Play.** Explore with your class all the variations on the verb *went*. Make a class chart of words that describe how a person can go from one place to another. Build the chart over the school year. Show students what some of the motions look like. Have students act out the ones they know. When the chart has as many words as children in the class, present a small play titled **Verb Play** or **The Way We Go,** or such, to another class. Have each student construct a large card to hold or wear as he or she pantomimes the action. Practice in the gym or on the playground at recess.

Sample list

amble	meander	stagger
clump	parade	stalk
crawl	plod	stamp
creep	prance	stomp
dance	race	stride
dash	run	stroll
flit	rush	strut
flounce	saunter	swagger
hop	scamper	tiptoe
inch along	shuffle	toddle
jog	sidle	traipse
limp	skedaddle	tramp
lope	skip	trot
lumber	slide	trudge
lurch	slink	waddle
march	sneak	wander

(Isn't it interesting how many movement words begin with the letter *S*?)

- **Sports Terms.** Have fourth graders bring in the sports sections of newspapers. (Ask colleagues to save the sports sections for you. Use them for students who do not have access to newspapers.) In peer partnerships, have students highlight the action words sportswriters use in headlines. Or cut out the words and create a collage. Students will find verbs, such as *blank, trounce, maul, wins, gets, lead, capture, stops, rallies, defend, sign, split, down, upset, surpasses, host, tied,* etc.

Try It Out in Writing (grades K–4)

1. **Kindergarten and first grade:** Using the cover of a mentor text or a large picture, take your students through a shared writing experience to describe the picture. Help them construct sentences that tell what is happening. Write their descriptions of the picture on chart paper. Have them read it chorally when it is finished.

On subsequent days, invite students to write independently, using *what's happening* as a Target Skill. Place action pictures in a Writing Center along with a laminated, small version of the stick-figure verb chart.

2. **Kindergarten through fourth grade:** Model strong-verb writing about a book cover or picture during the starting component of a subsequent daily writing workshop. After you model, have children write practice pieces of their own with *what's happening* or *strong verbs* as the Target Skill.

Kindergarten student tells what his dog does.

3. **First through fourth grade:** As the starting component of another writing workshop session, have students hold knee-to-knee conferences to tell their partners all about *what's happening* in pictures they select. Alternatively, you might ask them to make a list of all the action words—verbs—that apply to their pictures before they write. Talking and listing are great prewriting activities for all writers.

Students should then write independently about their pictures. Encourage them to include some sentences about *what is happening*, the Target Skill for the piece.

After writing, have the young writers read their pieces to partners. Provide stickers for first through fourth graders to place on their partners' papers where they hear action words. Explain that this is another version of *thumbs-up*. After peer conferences, call on partners to tell the class about another writer's use of action words in sentences. "Who gave a sticker for an action word you think we should all hear?" (*Building a Writing Community: A Practical Guide* and *Teaching the Youngest Writers: A Practical Guide* provide detailed descriptions of efficient peer conferencing and the use of compliment stickers.)

The Building
by
Nicholas, grade 4

I stand in the city beside a building surrounded by a fence of other buildings. This building is exceptionally special. It has a cross section of a triangle and is nine stories high. The smell of fumes is in the air. A flag sways above my head. With the cars zooming by and the people in suits holding briefcases you really get the feeling you're in a city.

Fourth grader focuses on verbs.

Practice and Application (grades 2–4)

- **Revision:** Have second to fourth graders read through their collections of practice pieces from past writing sessions. Ask them to look for Dinky Sentences they might have written. Remember, Dinky Sentences start with *There is, This is, He is, We have, We are, It is, It was, She has,* etc., and are usually short as well. Examples: *This is my dog. It is hot. We went to the zoo.* When students find some of them, make it seem like a great thing—"Good job editing!" Enthusiastically invite students who have found one to come to the board and write their sentences.

  Now, model how to replace Dinky Sentences with Good Writing, using action words: *My dog is chewing on my shoe. The sun was burning us up. We rode on a bus to the zoo.* Ask the students at the board to invite another student to the board, as a consultant, to help revise their Dinky Sentences at the board. Remind students that the best start to their sentences is a person, place, or thing (a noun) that then *does* something.

- **Independent writing:** Have students write descriptive pieces about a personal topic and call for the use of *strong verbs* as the Target Skill. In their peer conferences, have young writers reward each other's use of strong verbs with stickers or highlighting.

Diagnose and Assess (grades 1–4)

Diagnose your students' ability to use strong verbs by looking through their practice pieces. Make anecdotal notes in their records—the date that strong verbs appear at all, the date when they appear consistently. Conduct group lessons for students who need additional instruction in the skill. Always add complimentary comments about attempts to use Target Skills or to use them creatively. Young writers need encouragement. Writing is not easy.

Assess the use of *strong verbs* in an assigned and independent piece after ample practice opportunities. After discussions with your young writers about the quality or strength of verbs (e.g., "Is *went* a strong verb in our third grade class?"), apply a quality factor to your assessment of verb use. You can do this for all Target Skills.

When you assess children's writing, assess it only for the Target Skill(s) under study.

2. Descriptive Attributes and Adjectives (grades K–4)

After you establish strong-verb writing as a top priority, introduce your students to a variety of descriptive attributes, selecting the ones appropriate for your grade level as Target Skills from the list on page 44.

In kindergarten, *color, number,* and *shape* are good first targets. In first grade, add *size, texture, location,* and so forth. Select the attributes that complement what students are doing in math, science, art, music, and reading.

Introduce the Concept (Awareness) (grades K–4)

Before you begin to use *descriptive attributes* as Target Skills, play "I SPY" with your class. Model as many different attributes as you can. *I spy something red. I spy a circle. I spy something round. I spy something made of wood. I spy something furry.* Next, ask children to be IT to say: I SPY... Their classmates guess what they spied.

Play I SPY on the playground as well. Play it at the class easel, using a large art print or a Shared Reading Text cover.

Models from Books (grades K–4)

Reread nonfiction books and text you and your students have previously shared to look for examples of descriptive attributes. When students identify a specific adjective, ask them what general attribute they think it belongs to. For example: pink/*color,* fluffy/*texture,* tiny/*size,* six-legged/*number,* moist/*condition,* backyard/*location,* and so forth. Classmates might get into debates about which adjectives go with which attribute. Great. Young writers should discuss words and play with language.

Show students examples of descriptive attributes in storybooks as well, to demonstrate how important description is to all writing.

A Sampler of Descriptive Attributes

movement or action: creep, pounce, gurgle; present participle form: is gliding, is slithering, is flapping; *comparative*—faster, more frenzied, ...

color: purple, green, pale yellow; *comparative*—reddish, sea green, ...

size: nine by twelve inches, one hundred yards; *comparative*—larger, as big as, ...

shape: round, oval, cubic, square; *comparative*—columnar, tubular, triangular, ...

number: fourteen, a thousand; nonspecific—many, some, several; *comparative*—more than, fewer, ...

texture: smooth, rough, bumpy, lumpy, soft, fuzzy, slippery; *comparative*—stickier, slickest, ...

composition: wooden, metal, plastic, cloth, glass, concrete, cardboard, paper, ...

condition: wet, soaked, moist, dry, wrinkled, bent, twisted, ...

smell: smoky, putrid, floral, acrid, burnt, sweet; *comparative*—like smoke

taste: sweet, salty, acidic; *comparative*—like licorice, fruitier, ...

direction: left, right, up, down, backward, forward, ...

age: five years old, eighteen months old; nonspecific—old, new, ancient, antique; *comparative*—older than Methuselah, ...

weight: ten pounds, seven grams; nonspecific—heavy, light; *comparative*—as heavy as, the lightest, ...

special features: writing, designs, knobs, buttons, ...

symmetry: horizontal, vertical, radial

habitat: underground, forest, wetland, ocean, desert, ...

orientation: horizontal, vertical, parallel, perpendicular, ...

state: liquid, solid, gas

temperature: forty-six degrees, three below zero; nonspecific—broiling, freezing; *comparative*—hotter than, coldest, ...

Capstone nonfiction mentor texts
rich in adjectives:

> **A Baby Rabbit Story (SRT)**
>
> **A Baby Sea Otter Story (SRT)**
>
> **Animals with No Eyes**
>
> **Coral Reefs: Colorful Underwater Habitats (SRT)**
>
> **Countries Around the World: Costa Rica**
>
> **Countries Around the World: India**
>
> **Countries Around the World: Iran**
>
> **Desert Animal Adaptations**
>
> **Flesh-Eating Machines**
>
> **Look Inside a Tree**
>
> **Meat-Eating Plants and Other Extreme Plant Life**
>
> **Ocean Animal Adaptations (SRT)**
>
> **Polar Animal Adaptations (SRT)**
>
> **Using Your Senses (SRT)**
>
> **Which Seed Is This? (SRT)**

Try It Out Orally (grades K–4)

Attribute Show and Tell

The day before this activity, ask your young writers to bring in a colorful item. Make a set of attribute cards appropriate for the children's experience and background. Use attributes from the list on page 44: *color, shape, size, number, texture,* etc.

Conduct a Show and Tell. Children should tell about their objects, using as many of the attribute cards as they can. Or play it as a game with classmates holding up an attribute card and the player making up a sentence about the object using the attribute. For example, the color card is held up and the child with the object says, "My toy car is blue." Or do it the other way around: A child says something about the object, and the class identifies which attribute the child told about. For example, "My toy car zooms." The class guesses the attribute, *movement.*

Colors

Author Diane Ackerman points out in *A Natural History of the Senses* that we have a wide vocabulary of descriptive words for our sense of sight compared to a limited one for our senses of smell and taste. Apart from *putrid, fragrant, pungent, acrid, sour, sweet, bitter, tart,* and a few others, most of the words for smell and taste make a comparison to something else: *It smells like licorice, it smells like burnt leaves, it tastes like carrots.*

Words for colors are plentiful. Use the biggest box of crayons to demonstrate the variety. Show children how many color names use comparisons to natural elements, such as flowers, trees, and woods—*periwinkle blue, coral, primrose, lemon yellow, mahogany, sky blue, orchid, ash blond,* etc.

Provide color-word resources for students. Ask your art teacher for other sources in addition to the following:

- Box of 64 crayons
- Paint strips: Dozens of cards each with an array of 6–8 named shades of one color are available at paint and hardware stores. (Mary Beth's first graders at Dunbar Magnet School, Tampa, FL, keep paint strips in a pocket chart. They have labeled each pocket a basic color: BLUES, REDS, YELLOWS, etc. If they cannot read the color name on a strip when Mary Beth has her Editor's Hat on (the class signal that no one can interrupt her and the student she is helping), they just make up a new name for the color from what it reminds them of: Pea-soup green, Cheerios yellow, Bayside blue. They have even renamed their table groups using some of their made-up color names.)
- Carpet samples: Sets of 4" x 4" pieces, in an array of named colors and shades (These are especially appealing to primary students who love to run their hands over the carpet.)
- New car color charts from local car dealers

Textures

Create a collection of textures. Mount samples of fur, carpet, velvet, sandpaper, vinyl, Velcro, etc., on Masonite panels or heavy card stock. Invite students to add other samples. Make a class chart of words to describe these textures. Use children's words first, even made-up words. Add to the chart as you and your young writers find a texture word when you read aloud to them. Place students' initials after their contributions to the chart.

Shapes

Integrate geometry and writing by using plane and three-dimensional shapes as descriptive vocabulary. Once you have introduced geometric shapes to the children in math, take your writers on a short field trip in the schoolyard to find those shapes in the natural and architectural environment. Set a limited goal of finding and describing two geometric shapes. Model talking about geometric shapes before you go outside.

I see a triangle. It is the slide and the ladder and the ground.

The red sign in front of the school is a square.

Use a "shape check-off sheet" for kindergarten and first graders. (See the chart below.)

On a field trip outside, have kids draw things that have those shapes. When you return to class, construct a class chart through shared writing, compiling the students' contributions. (See page 52 for what some first graders did.)

Shape or features	I see
Round ○	
Square □	
Triangle △	
Striped ___	
Dotted ° ° °	
Crossed ✕	

Schoolyard Field Trip Hints

When you take your primary students out to the playground, attach a long string to your belt. Give the end of the string to a student and have all the students line up behind him. Ask the leader to keep the string extended as far as it will go. Then ask the group to start walking in a large circle around you, following the student holding the end of the string. When they have completed the circle, tell them they must all stay within that circle's distance from you during the field trip in the yard. Then remove the string.

Sounds

Compared to sights, we have a limited vocabulary for sounds. We expand it by making up words that imitate sounds. *splash, whir, pbzzt, kerplop.* A word imitating a sound is called **onomatopoeia,** pronounced on´ a mat´ a pee´ a. Children love to learn and say big, juicy words like this. Don't be shy about using big words with your little students.

The Capstone mentor texts, ***Polar Animal Adaptations*** and ***If I Were a Veterinarian,*** start with sound words, or onomatopoeia, as a hook technique. Young writers can make up their own sound spellings. Great models for doing that are Peter Spier's books about onomatopoeia, ***Crash! Bang! Boom!,*** and ***Gobble, Growl, Grunt.***

We can describe sounds by their source and intensity as well as their quality. Take your class outside for a sound field trip. Seat the class in a comfortable spot and ask youngsters to identify one or two sounds. *Can you describe it? Where does it come from? Is it loud or soft? Is it pretty or is it annoying?* **This is an oral exercise.** Later, provide a selection of pictures, or have students draw some, that have a noise element to them. Example: a parade, a baseball game, a washing machine, an animal.

Invite the children to use sound words in their writing, making them up if they need to. When you read to your class, show students when an author uses onomatopoeia. Write the word on the board or a class chart of noise words. Pronounce the word for your students and have them pronounce it.

Try It Out in Writing (grades K–4)

Model descriptive writing often for your students. Show how you chose the attributes you think are important to your reader, the ones that are important to you, the ones that dominate a scene or situation. Think aloud as you make these choices and construct your text.

Have children try out writing descriptively after they are comfortable with attributes and have *talked* description using strong verbs and attributes. Later, add the use of comparisons to their describing techniques. (See next section: 3. Descriptive Comparisons.)

Kindergarten and First Grade

Encourage students to use color, number, and action words when they write independently about their drawings. In Author's Chair, have classmates give colorful stickers to writers who use these attributes. The writers and compliment givers will place them beside the attribute words (written at all levels: strings of letters with no sound-to-symbol connection, consonants representing words, beginning and end consonant for a word, transitional spelling of a word).

Attribute Hunt (grades 1–4)

Take students on an attribute hunt inside or outside the school building. Provide clipboards or squares of whiteboard and markers for writing. Before the students start their quest, model talking and writing about attributes in sentence form. *I see a leaf the size of a nickel. The swings are taller than the trees.*

Or, provide a form with attributes listed, such as the following.

Attribute Hunt

Find something outside in nature for each attribute: Describe it in just <u>one</u> sentence.

Example: Size: *I found a leaf that is as <u>tiny</u> as a bug.* Or *The brook by the library is about <u>six feet across</u>.*

Movement: _____

Color: _____

Shape: _____

Number: _____

Location: _____

Made of: _____

Smell: _____

Texture: _____

Weight: (as heavy as ...) _____

Sound: _____

Symmetry: _____

Art Gallery (grades 2–4)

Post art prints, photographs, and mentor texts with interesting covers around your classroom or in an adjacent hallway, gallery style. As a starting component to writing workshop have students stroll through the gallery. Ask them to choose the picture they like best. Then, in partners, have them take turns standing in front of their choices and telling each other all about the pictures. Rove and encourage. Gather a group of students who

might not be able to succeed at the task in this format. Take them around the room with you and do the exercise together. Model, and ask for, a *thumbs-up* during students' descriptions.

Meet to share as a whole group. Invite students to write about the picture they described. They may do this standing in front of their picture choice.

Boxing
by
Jed

In this art picture it is very smokey inside the building. People can bet on the fighters and may even bet on the one that is laying on the ground. Some people are crushed all because the fighter is on the ground.

People are raising hands and saying, "Get up, get up" to the boxer but he can't because he is knocked out. He is raising his hand too.

And I think that they are ready to ring the bell but he might get up. You never know.

Fourth grader's review of an art print.

Practice and Assessment (grades 1–4)

- Explore attributes with your students by listing all the adjectives that apply to one attribute. For example, have them make a list or a class chart in shared writing of all the words that represent movement, sound, size, or temperature. Older students can place these words on a continuum, arranging the words from one extreme to another. For example: *broiling, roasting. boiling, hot, warm, cool, chilly, icy, freezing.*

- Assign various attributes as Target Skills in Writing Centers, for homework journaling, or in a current independent piece. Use students' practice writes to diagnose for group review needs.

- After ample practice, students' work may be assessed for specific attribute application.

I like the way the
artist did the sky.
It looks like he wetted it
with a brush sweep of
water. So when he painted
with water colors X
it sped like melted
butter on hot tost.
I love the backround.

Second grader's review of a Monet painting.

Publish Attribute Books

Attribute books focus on one attribute and give illustrations of it—*red is for apples, red is for fire trucks, red is for stop.* Or, they focus on one object and give all its attributes—*apples are red, apples are round, apples are yummy.* Writers of all ages enjoy making attribute books. They can be presented as shape books, too.

3. Descriptive Comparisons (grades K–4)

Professional writers help their readers visualize scenes and objects by comparing one thing to something else. They use a variety of techniques to do this. Young writers can employ these same techniques. They are listed here in order of increasing difficulty for children. Introduce one at a time, over the course of the year in all grades. Point them out when you read aloud, and use them in your writing models.

- Use words with the suffixes **er** or **est:**
  bigger, kinder, the oldest
  Brian plays Nintendo better than his dad.

- Use the word **like:**
  That dog looks like my dog. Their ears droop way down.

- Use the phrase **just like:**
  My mom cooks spaghetti just like Tony's mom.

- Use a **simile:** The simile form is, **as** _____
  as _____ .
  The worm crawls as slow as a snail.

- Use the phrase **reminds me of:**
  The girl in that book reminds me of my best friend.

Capstone titles that illustrate *descriptive comparisons (er and est, like, just like, reminds me of, so X that, simile):*

All about Boats *(earliest, larger, like fire trucks, so cold it freezes over, like a snowplow on water, like taking a vacation on a floating hotel)*

Big, Bigger, Biggest *(so small they can hardly be seen, so big they are giant, taller, about the same as 100 second graders, bigger, like an elephant, largest, as big as)*

Countries Around the World: Costa Rica *(smaller than the state of West Virginia, most, largest industry, most active, warmest, most active, as far away as, most valuable, most biodiverse, largest butterflies, piglike, highest literacy rate, smallest villages)*

Countries Around the World: India *(poorest, richer, earliest, largest, cheapest, biggest, faster, More films are made in India than anywhere else in the world, good players are as popular as film stars, most popular, India's population is growing faster than China's)*

Countries Around the World: Iran *(one of the oldest civilizations on Earth, greatest, greater variety of jobs, more than half, newer words, largest province, fourth-largest producer of oil, fifth-largest producer of natural gas, most, most popular)*

Desert Animal Adaptations *(jumbo sized, like shoes, scooplike hands, yak's jacket, woolly underwear, lighter)*

From Mealworm to Beetle (SRT) *(about the same size as, as long as, last as long as, longer, a bit longer)*

Long and Short (SRT) *(longer than a minivan, shorter than a jelly bean, longest, shortest, longer than its body, longest insects)*

Polar Animal Adaptations (SRT) *(like giant freezers, warmest, tube-shaped, best, fuzzy slippers, longer, bigger, act like snowshoes, like giant teeth, warmer)*

The Attractive Truth about Magnetism *(like a super hero; latest; like curved lines; metaphor: Earth is one giant magnet; bigger; stronger; closer; tiniest; so small that you can't see them; smallest; like the center)*

Welcome to Mexico *(like a tornado, like a triangle, most famous, largest city)*

Which Seed Is This? (SRT) *(size of a dinner plate, shaped like hearts, tallest, like teeth)*

Introduce the Concept (Awareness) (grades K–4)

Show your students a pinecone or an apple. Ask them to describe it to someone who has never seen one. Suggest that a good way to do that would be to compare it to something the person might already be familiar with.

Model a sentence that describes by comparison only. For example, say, *A pinecone is as big as a potato. It is brown like a shoe.* Or *Apples are bigger than plums. An apple is red like a fire engine.* Ask your students for other sentences that describe the pinecone or apple by showing that it is similar to something almost everyone would know. Compare by color, size, shape, and feel, i.e., as many attributes as possible.

Model this skill often. Exercises of this nature reinforce children's observational skills and logical thinking.

Models from Books (grades K–4)

Use examples from the listed mentor texts to show students how authors use comparisons to tell their readers what things are like or look like, and how they feel, move, etc. ***Big, Bigger, Biggest*** is rich in comparison types. You will find examples, such as *bigger, so big that, so small that, about the same as, largest, as long as.* ***Polar Animal Adaptations*** illustrates several forms of comparisons, including metaphor. Read from ***More Similes: Roar Like a Lion*** by Joan Hanson and ***AS: A Surfeit of Similes*** by Norton Juster. Make a chart list of the various ways authors make comparisons.

Try It Out Orally

<u>er</u> and <u>est</u>: (grades K–3)

The youngest writers can start by creating and saying simple comparisons using *er* and *est.* Provide photographs, laminated magazine pictures, or covers of informational mentor texts for children to choose from and to prompt their comparisons. Model several for your students: *A fire engine is bigger than a taxi. A fire engine is taller than a car.*

Then have them make comparisons using *er* and *est* to describe things in pictures they select. Some children will use similes naturally: *The dog is as tall as the boy.* When you find children who can compare in this fashion, compliment them and support them with a lesson about similes. Encourage them to use similes in their independent writing.

Like (grades K–4)

Encourage young writers to compose a fresh and vivid comparison by asking them questions such as, "What did it **look like** to you? What did it **seem like** to you?" Emphasize the word, *like.*

> *The cars are crawling like ants.*
> *It's sticky like pancake syrup.*

Follow shared reading with shared writing experiences to create lists of examples pertaining to the students in your classroom. Tie the comparisons to the study of movement and verbs: *John can swim as fast as an otter. Carla can hop like a kangaroo. Nathan can sing as loud as a trumpet.* (See page 51, A First Grade's Study of Attributes and Comparisons.)

Try It Out in Writing (grades K–4)

Michelle's first graders, Dunbar Magnet School, Tampa, FL, took a description field trip to the schoolyard to observe cloud formations. Michelle began to describe clouds: "That cloud looks like …" The children continued, saying what they thought clouds looked like. Upon returning to class, the children made "clouds" by folding blue paper in half, dropping white paint from an eyedropper on one half, then folding the paper back together. After a few minutes they opened their papers to see what their "clouds" looked like.

On the following day, Michelle used the Target Skill, *comparison,* in modeled writing. She showed her students how to put the letters *C* for comparison at the top of their writing paper to remind them of the target. The children then wrote about their paint clouds. As you can see from their work (see page 50), they also put *M* for movement, an earlier Target Skill, on their papers.

On a subsequent day, Michelle conducted a shared writing in which students combined both movement and comparisons Target Skills to make a class chart like this:

Name	Verb	Compare
Tamika	runs	like a deer.
Derrick	walks	like a turtle.
Mylin	jumps	like a bunny.
Brianne	swims	like a shark.

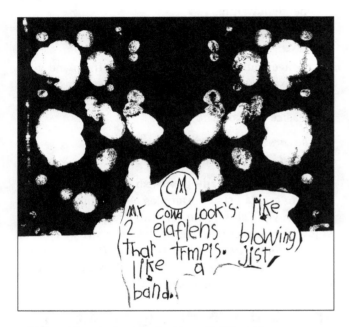

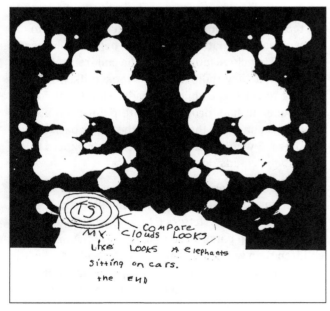

Next, the students made a class book. They drew pictures of animals performing a movement from the class chart. They placed small school photos of themselves in place of the heads of the animals. Then they wrote their comparative sentences on the page. (See a similar sample from the children's class book above.)

- **Shared writing:** In kindergarten and first grade, help your students use comparisons in a class descriptive piece. Place a large photograph or shared reading mentor text on the easel and have the children describe people and objects in the cover photo. Then help them compose a class description of the photo on chart paper. Remind them of the different ways to make comparisons.

- **Revision opportunity:** If, in the shared writing, a child uses an adjective but not a comparison, write it as the child dictates it. When the piece is complete, bring the class back to the adjective and show how they can create a simile in its place. You will be modeling revision as well.

For example, if the sentence is *The kids are blowing big bubbles,* ask your young writers to look at the word *big.* Ask, "How big are the bubbles? As big as apples? As big as basketballs? Would they look big to an ant? an elephant? How big exactly?" Cross out the word *big*, then insert, as *big as basketballs,* after the word *bubbles. The kids are blowing bubbles as big as basketballs.* Ask your students to demonstrate bubbles as big as basketballs with their arms and hands. Ask them if they think that the comparison helps the reader visualize the bubbles, as opposed to just saying they are *big.*

- **Model** a short description of a picture from your photo collection or the cover of a Shared Reading Text. Use every kind of comparison technique you can. Show students examples by other young writers who have practiced the skill.

• **Older students** can work in groups to make lists of sentences using *like* and using similes. Collate their lists and publish the collection for them to keep in their writing notebooks.

Never Too Much

Do not be afraid to model excessive use of a technique, even to the point of ridiculousness. Later in independent writing, students invariably will use it less than in a practice piece. The exercise is comparable to practicing basketball foul shots. You may shoot 50–100 foul shots in practice; but in a game you'll shoot three or four, if you are lucky.

Comparisons☺

Justin
Practice
This is a picture of a cawala bear and his eyes are like marballs.
His claws are so sharp they would probily dig right into a tree.
His fur looks a little hard.
He is as small as a cereal box.

(Grade 2)

• **Writing/Science and Social Studies Field Trips.** Incorporate the use of comparisons in the descriptive writing students do in the content areas. Use your schoolyard (and encourage students to investigate their own neighborhoods) as an area to observe and describe.

Practice and Application (grades 2–4)

Make *comparisons* a Target Skill for the writing students to do throughout the week in homework journaling. Display a chart of the various comparison techniques. Write anecdotal notes about each child's progress. Conduct group lessons to review the skill. In grades two through four, assign comparisons as a Target Skill in ongoing personal writing pieces. After students have had ample practice, assign comparisons as a Target Skill on a piece you will assess.

A First Grade's Study of Descriptive Attributes and Comparisons

Mary Beth, Dunbar Magnet School, Tampa, FL. conducted the following study over two weeks. Here is her description of the lessons and activities in her first grade class.

"First I introduced children to the concept of attributes through reading aloud and noting such things as color, shape, movement, size. Next, we had a toy celebration. Students described their toys while partners identified the attributes they used in their description. The descriptions were then listed on a class chart during a shared writing experience.

"Next, we read a science Shared Reading Text, focusing on the descriptions, especially the ones that used comparisons. We noted the words *like* and *as*, and called them *buzz* words. We built a chart of comparative phrases. We practiced making comparisons using a pinecone. (See 3. Descriptive Comparisons on page 48.)

"On the next day, I read the poem, *What the Animals Do*, which uses the word *like* to describe movement.

What the Animals Do

We'll hop, hop, hop like a bunny,
And run, run, run like a dog;
We'll walk, walk, walk like an elephant,
And jump, jump, jump like a frog;
We'll swim, swim, swim like a goldfish,
And fly, fly, fly like a bird;
We'll sit right down and fold our hands,
And not say a single word.

(Author unknown)

"We made up movements, and I built a class chart of stick figures to illustrate them. In addition, through shared writing, we made up a class list of the way each child moves, using comparisons. *Lesley sits as quiet as a mouse.* The children copied their entries and illustrated them.

"On another day, we read **Quick as a Cricket** by Audrey Wood and added phrases to our class chart of comparisons.

"During the next week we went into the schoolyard to record, by drawing or writing, the things in our schoolyard that had each attribute. I modeled this on the data sheet we would use before we went outside.

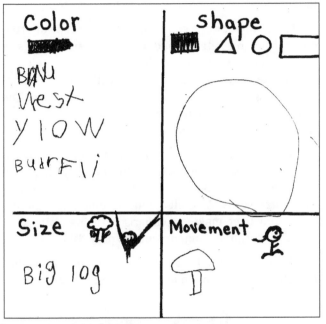

First grader's field trip notes.

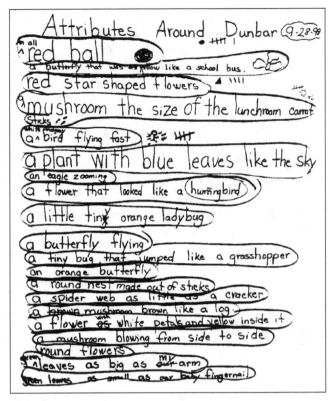

Class chart

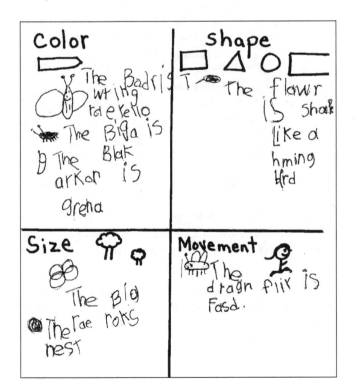

Definition of the Term *Compare*

The term compare is a bit tricky. You can compare things *to* each other or with *each* other.

When you compare one thing *to* another, you show how they are similar or different with regard to one attribute. In the preceding lesson, descriptive comparisons are used to compare things to each other. For example, the sentences, *The dog is bigger than the cat* and *Annie is a shrimp* compare the dog to the cat and Annie to a shrimp (only in terms of size).

When you compare things with each other, you analyze several of their attributes to show both similarities and differences. For example, If we compare cats with dogs, we can say both are mammals, have tails and whiskers, and are carnivores. They both have claws, but a cat's claws retract while a dog's doesn't. Cats purr but dogs bark, etc.

"On the next day I built a class chart, through shared writing, of the things my students saw and noted.

"Next, students wrote sentences, during **independent writing,** about what they saw outside. They could refer to the shared writing chart and their data sheets.

"After rereading our science Shared Reading Text to see how it was organized, we constructed a class book titled: *Our Attribute Walk.* We separated it into sections about color, shape, size, and movement in our schoolyard and built a table of contents."

Table of Contents

4. Contrast and Opposites (grades 1–4)

Authors use contrast or opposites for emphasis and for effect when they describe things. The contrast may serve to define the things described. For example, from a book about wetlands, the text, *Swamps have trees. Marshes don't.* is a succinct definitive difference.

Sentences, phrases, or words of contrast (antonyms) are usually placed close together for effect. Example of contrast: *Farmers milk their cows—by hand or by machine.* And: *The soft ice cream becomes firm in a very cold room.*

Capstone mentor texts that illustrate *contrast and antonyms:*

Comparing Materials (SRT)

Coral Reefs: Colorful Underwater Habitats (SRT)

Countries Around the World: Costa Rica

First Nations of North America: Northeast Indians

Instruments and Music

Let's Rock: Crystals

Polar Animal Adaptations (SRT)

The Terrible, Awful Civil War

Using Your Senses (SRT)

Weather Watchers: Weather (SRT)

Welcome to Mexico

What Is a Community? (SRT)

What Is a Family? (SRT)

Introduce the Concept (Awareness) (grades 1–4)

Introduce or review the concept of opposites and antonyms with your class. Use the cover of one of the mentor texts suggested to model sentences that use both types of opposites: positive and negative versions of a verb: *have* and *don't have, can* and *can't,* and specific antonyms: *wet* and *dry, up* and *down, over* and *under.*

For example, using a book about gardening, students can suggest sentences, such as: *The carrots and corn are long, but the radishes and onions are short. The carrots, radishes, and onion all grow under the ground and the corn grows above the ground, on the cornstalk.*

Models from Books

Read one of the suggested mentor texts that illustrate the use of contrast and antonyms. Stop and point out the examples. Read others and have students give a *thumbs-up* signal when they see or hear examples of opposites.

In a shared writing session, make a class chart for the pairs of opposites young writers think up or find in a mentor text or in their other reading. Publish the class list for second, third, and fourth graders to put in their writer's notebooks. Encourage students to use the list when they write independently.

Try It Out Orally (grades 1–4)

- Play word games with your young students to study antonyms. Include acting out opposites.
- Have students in small groups draw or paste pictures of pairs of things that show contrast or opposites. Your model for this exercise might be pictures or objects.
  — black bear and polar bear: black and white
  — basketball and a baseball: large and small
  — desert and jungle: dry and damp
  — a skyscraper and a one-story building: tall and short
  — plastic baggy and paper toweling: smooth and rough
  — a sidewalk and a winding road: straight and curved

Conduct a sharing session. As the groups or partners display their drawing or pictures and report their antonyms, write the antonyms under each picture to reinforce the concept.

Try It Out in Writing (grades 1–4)

Flip Books (grades mid-1–4)

Through the use of flip books, children can practice comparing things **with** each other and then focus on the **differences** to practice contrast: opposites (antonyms). A concrete object, such as a flip book, enhances the comparing experience for many students. Venn diagrams are also a useful tool. You will find many examples in professional education resources (magazine and books) of how to make Venn diagrams with such concrete materials as hula hoops or circles of rope or yarn.

Part I: Brainstorming a List of Pairs

Begin your lesson about contrast (which should be stretched out over several days) by brainstorming with the class to create a list of **pairs that are similar.** List several entries to get the class started. Use real objects with the younger students: toys, foods, utensils, and such. When the class list has 10 or more entries, invite your students to tell one reason the pairs of things are alike and one reason they are different. Write their responses after each pair on the list. Compliment them on their work. You might take two days or more to complete this list.

Here is a list collected from a second grade class:

- dog and cat—both are furry, a dog's tongue is smooth and a cat's is scratchy
- duck and chicken—both are birds, a duck's feet are webbed and a chicken's aren't
- lake and ocean—both are big bodies of water, a lake is fresh water and an ocean is salty
- horse and cow—both are farm animals, a cow has horns and a horse doesn't
- fire engine and ambulance—both have sirens, a fire engine has hoses but an ambulance doesn't
- nickel and quarter—both are coins, a nickel has a smooth edge and a quarter has a bumpy edge
- *The Three Little Pigs* and *Goldilocks and the Three Bears*—both are books with three of the same animals, there's a girl in *Goldilocks and the Three Bears* but no girl in *The Three Little Pigs*
- whales and fish—both live in the ocean, whales are mammals and fish aren't
- library and bookstore—both have books, you borrow a book from the library and you buy a book from a bookstore
- snake and worm—both are long and skinny, a snake has a tongue but a worm doesn't
- doctor and dentist—both are doctors, a dentist is for your teeth and a doctor is for all of you

Part II: Making the Book

A flip book is an easily constructed, concrete aid for making comparisons. It's small enough to fit a child's hand and is easily carried about in a pocket. Children like to make flip books themselves after you show them how. Here's how:

Materials: 8-1/2" x 11" sheets of unlined paper for each student and an 11" x 14" sheet of construction paper for your model.

Directions: Fold the large sheet of paper in front of the class, as follows. Go slowly and repeat the procedure. Then start again and ask children to fold their papers in the same fashion.

- Fold a sheet of unlined paper to look like a hot dog bun.
- Hold the paper vertically and fold the top down toward yourself to look like a hamburger roll.
- Fold that down toward yourself again, to look like half a peanut butter sandwich.
- Unfold the paper back to its hot dog bun shape. Open the sheet and drape it over arm, so it looks like a rooftop.
- Cut each fold line **up side only,** to the top of the roof.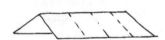

Part III Using the Flip Books to Show Contrast

Talk about one of the pairs from the class list. Set up a chart on the blackboard/whiteboard or a large sheet of paper to enter information about the pair as the class compares one with the other. The individuals occupy the vertical axis, and the attributes occupy the horizontal axis of the chart.

Such a chart is also called a table. Building a table like the one on the next page helps children organize information. Model and build tables often. Organizing data is a critical thinking skill. (See also Chapter 5, Presenting Information Graphically: Charts)

Note: You will have to name the subcategories or attributes that form the column titles, as primary children are not able to do this abstract task. With plenty of practice at the General-to-Specific Game and making lists, they will begin to do this subcategorizing independently around the fourth and fifth grade.

Chart

	Beak	Head	Feet	Food	Live	Noise	Babies
Duck	round/flat	smooth	webbed	pond weeds	water/pond	quack	ducklings
Chicken	pointy	red comb	toes	grain	land, farm	cluck, peep	chicks

Flip Book

Draw a flip book on the board as a model, or use your large one made of heavy paper. On the flip book, write about one of the pairs on a top flap of the booklet. Under the flap, write about the second of the pair, **contrasting** it (showing how it is different) to the first of the pair in terms of the same attribute. *Ducks have webbed feet. Chickens don't.*

Point out to your students that you focused on the way the duck and the chicken are **different** by looking at some attributes: their feet, where they live, their beaks, and their heads. Then you wrote, using antonyms to tell how they were different, or even opposite, in each attribute.

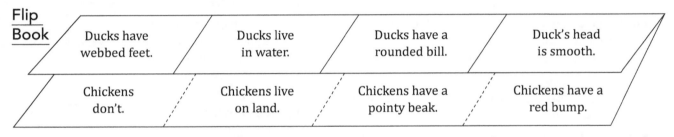

Flip Book

Ducks have webbed feet. / Ducks live in water. / Ducks have a rounded bill. / Duck's head is smooth.

Chickens don't. / Chickens live on land. / Chickens have a pointy beak. / Chickens have a red bump.

Trying It Out in Writing (grades 2-4)

Invite your young writers to make a chart like the one you modeled about a pair they want to compare and describe. Do not be dismayed if some students copy your work exactly—which is what often happens during modeling. Remember, this is practice. The act of copying your model will help them fix the concept in their minds.

Copy the Pros

Gary Provost, in *100 Ways to Improve Your Writing* (New American Library, NY, 1989) advises writers that it's OK to copy. It's fine to copy a few paragraphs from a book word for word. In doing so, you become aware of an author's craft, i.e., the choices the author made.

Next, have students use a flip book. Children should work in partners as they draw or write only about the **differences,** the contrast, between their pairs. Encourage them to talk as they work.

As with all introductory lessons, many children will not be good at the task. Repeat the lesson throughout the school year. Show them writing samples in which other young writers used contrast. (You will want to make a collection of student writing illustrating the writing-craft skills you teach. Children are impressed with writing by a kid like them. Your models should come from both professional writing and children's writing.)

Practice and Application (grades 2-4)

- Assign the use of contrast (antonyms) as a Target Skill in content-area homework journaling. Model sample entries for students. *Lakes are bodies of water surrounded by land. They can be small enough to swim across. They can be so large you cannot see across them.*

- Model a literature response to fiction that focuses on the contrast between the main character and the reader or between two main characters. *Henry Huggins has a bike but I don't; The wolf was mean but the woodsman was nice; Jack is a small boy. On the other hand, the Giant is huge.* Then, have students respond to literature in a similar fashion.

- Make contrast the Target Skill in a piece of ongoing writing. In peer conferences ask students to identify where another student has used contrast and to reward the author with compliment stickers or highlighting.

B. Engaging the Reader (grades 1–4)

If we want to hold our readers' attention, we must write in a lively and engaging fashion. One way to do this is to speak directly to, or with, our readers, using the pronouns *I, you, we,* and *us.* One way to write in a dull and awkward manner is to consciously avoid using these pronouns. Unfortunately, in high school English most of us were told, erroneously, not to use *I, you, we,* and *us* in expository writing. Fortunately, writing experts now unanimously tell us that this was and is poor advice.

William Zinsser, a leading authority on nonfiction writing, in *Writing to Learn*[1], tells of John Rodgers, a distinguished professor of geology at Yale, who became so maddened by a fuzzy student dissertation that he composed and gave to his students a tongue-in-cheek manifesto, called "Rules of Bad Writing." One rule was: *Never use the first person where you can use ambiguous phrases like "the writer" or, "it is thought," or, better still, "it is considered by some," so the reader can't be exactly sure who thinks what, or what—if anything—you think.*

Additionally, Zinsser advises, "Writers should not hesitate to use the word **you**, even in a serious academic piece." The avoidance of **you** results in pompous writing, such as: *One can tell when one has entered a rain forest, when one feels that the air temperature has dropped several degrees due to the humid and shaded nature of these areas.* Change this sentence, using the active voice and the pronoun *you.* Say it to yourself and you will see immediately how much more engaging it is to talk directly with or to your reader.

[1]William Zinsser, *Writing to Learn.* (New York: Harper & Row, Publishers, 1988). p. 80.

Capstone mentor texts that illustrate the use of pronouns to engage readers:

All about Boats

Animals with No Eyes

Community Helpers

Everybody Moves

Fun at the Zoo

Magnetism: A Question and Answer Book

Meat-Eating Plants and Other Extreme Plant Life

Parks of the U.S.A.

Polar Animal Adaptations (SRT)

The Bloody, Rotten Roman Empire

The Dreadful, Smelly Colonies

The Terrible, Awful Civil War

Up North and Down South

Using Your Senses (SRT)

Weather Watchers: Weather (SRT)

Introduce the Concept (Awareness) (grades 1–4)

The best way to introduce this concept to young writers is to show them contrasting pieces about the same topic; one that talks directly to or with the reader, and another that does not. You will need to prepare sentence strips of text from one or several of the listed Capstone mentor texts and compose contrasting versions. Read the two versions to your students. (See some examples in the chart on page 58.)

Discuss with your students which versions talk to them and which ones just give information. Ask them which they prefer.

Models from Capstone Mentor Texts (grades 1–4)

Following the discussion, read one of the suggested informational mentor texts that illustrate using pronouns. Have students give a *thumbs-up* signal when they hear a sentence that talks directly to them.

Read other books from the list. Point out where the author uses the pronouns *I, you, we,* and *us* specifically to engage the reader.

This activity is a good opportunity to review the use of pronouns. Not only do writers use pronouns to replace people's names, they use them to *talk with* the reader.

Phrases that Engage Readers (grades 2–4)

Professional writers keep their own lists of useful phrases, or they refer to trade books that contain such things as dialogue tags, first lines, names, expressions, idioms, similes, etc. Young writers can copy the pros and keep lists of their own: strong verbs, attributes (colors, shapes, textures), hooks, endings, and even phrases that engage the readers.

The best lists are those the children build, like the class chart of verbs. These completed charts should also be printed for students in grades two and above to keep in their writer's notebooks. If you just give them a list that you have created, they will feel no sense of authorship, and it will go the way of all such papers.

Engaging the Reader	Not Engaging to the Reader
Magnetism: A Question and Answer Book	
Every day, we use magnets and magnetism in countless ways.	Magnets are used in many ways.
Your stereo speakers use magnets to change electric signals into sound.	In stereo speakers, magnets change electric signals into sound.
No matter how hard you try, a magnet won't pick up a U.S. penny.	A magnet will not pick up a U.S. penny.
The Terrible, Awful Civil War	
How would you like to go to school wearing a scratchy jacket, tattered pants, and worn shoes?	Civil War uniforms were uncomfortable.
Imagine being a Civil War soldier on the march for hours under a hot sun.	Marching was hot for Civil War soldiers.
Picture yourself living in a camp with hundreds of men and piles of waste all around.	War camps were crowded and dirty.

The following list, Sample Phrases that Engage Readers, is intended only for you as a guide to a similar one your students can build by finding examples in their reading or class shared reading.

Try It Out Orally (grades 1–4)

Asking questions of the reader or saying *I think* are two easy ways for young writers to begin using phrases to engage their reader. Use photo cards or magazine pictures in a whole-class setting to model how to engage the reader. For example, using the cover of **Everybody Moves**, you might say: *Have you ever used a hula hoop? I think it must be very difficult to get it started. Maybe it has to do with turning your body. Look at how the girl has turned her shoulders.*

Invite your students to tell about their pictures in this fashion, asking their readers an occasional question. Model this for the whole class first. In the next writing session, show them how to do it in a peer conference.

Try It Out in Writing (grades 1–4)

- In shared writing, have your students compose a paragraph about a large picture clipped to a sheet of chart paper. Encourage them to start some of their sentences with a question to their reader or to begin with the phrase *I think*. Write the sentences they contribute under the picture. Have them read it with you as you write, and again when it is completed.

- In modeled writing, show how to *ask questions* or use *I think* and others phrases from the class chart of engaging phrases. Use a large picture and invite your students to compose in tandem with you. For example, everyone starts with the phrase *I think...*, and writes his or her own sentence. Select a second engaging phrase and again have everyone write his or her own version. When you have used four or five phrases, have everyone share his or her piece with a partner. Invite young writers to tell the class which examples they heard that they think everyone else would like to hear as well—peers complimenting peers.

Sample Phrases that Engage Readers

Pronouns

I wonder ...

I think ...

To my surprise ...

I was amazed to see (hear) ...

If you think ...

You should see how ...

You'd be surprised ...

You can hear ...

You can see ...

You can tell ...

If you look ...

We can ...

All of us ...

Imperative Statements—Reader, do something

Picture ...

Look closely ...

Listen ...

Watch ...

Examine ...

Watch out for ...

Study ...

Questions

Did you ever wonder ...?

Can you imagine ...?

Have you ever ...?

Could it be ...?

What do you think ...?

During independent writing, have your young writers use the engaging phrases in a short practice piece, perhaps picture-prompted. When they finish, have them meet in peer conferences to read their work to other writers. They should give each other stickers or highlight the places where they have used a phrase to engage their readers. Later, ask some of the writers to tell the class about phrases they complimented in their classmates' writing.

Sea World

You should go to this fun and enormous theme park named Sea World! Sea World is so fun that you'd want to go there again. Keeping you entertained as your birthday keeps you entertained is what Sea World does.

Inside Sea world is a really cool water roller coaster that runs on steel tracks. Journey to Atlantis is the name of the coaster, because it takes you through the lost city of Atlantis. Journey to Atlantis is a big building with an adventure inside and a coaster outside. After you go through the cool city you're really high, as high as three stories! Then you find yourself sliding down so fast like a rock thrown from a airplane! It does this twice. Sea World is a blast (a horror at first)!

Come watch Shamu! He's smooth and is black like a night without a moon and has white spots. In a show Shamu can splash up to seven benches in one splash! If you're in the first seven benches get ready to be splashed with salty water! In Sea World Shamu is pretty famous. Will you be going to Sea World one day?

Nancy

Fourth grader engages her readers.

Practice and Application (grades 1–4)

- Encourage first graders to use the phrase *I think* when they write about personal topics or pictures. In late first grade, introduce the *question* hook as a way to engage the reader.

- Make *Engaging the Reader* a Target Skill for all writing that older students do throughout the day. Post it as a Target Skill in a writing center. When students write independently in writing workshop or in their homework writing journals, assign the use of an engaging phrase as a Target Skill.

- Have students build class or individual charts of engaging phrases as they find examples in their independent reading.

- Provide second through fourth graders with a collection of magazine or newspaper texts and have them highlight any *Engaging the Reader* phrases they find.

Assessment

Add *Engaging the Reader* to the list of criteria for evaluating student writing (grades 2–4) in several independent pieces. If you use state writing assessment criteria, such as organization, focus, elaboration, conventions, voice, purpose, and sentence variation when you assess writing for grading purposes, add your own specific craft skills to the criteria list in the categories to which they apply. Most of the writing skills described in this book correspond to the Common Core State Standards. As with all writing assessment, students must know what the criteria are when they submit writing for your evaluation.

C. Alliteration (grades K–4)

When children list words that all start with the same sound in phonics practice, they are using a literary technique called *alliteration*. Authors deliberately place two words starting with the same sound next to each other for the appealing sound it creates. Children's authors are particularly adept at this, deliberately using alliteration to make their writing sound melodic when it is read aloud. You will find models in fiction and in well-written informational books.

Capstone mentor texts that illustrate *alliteration:*

Animal Migration

Countries Around the World: Costa Rica

Desert Animal Adaptations

First Nations of North America: Great Basin Indians

Flesh-Eating Machines

Let's Rock: Fossils

Look Inside a Tree

Ocean Animal Adaptations (SRT)

Polar Animal Adaptations (SRT)

The Crude, Unpleasant Age of Pirates

The Life Cycle of Birds

Introduce the Concept (Awareness) (grades K–4)

Introduce your children to alliteration by immersing them in it. Read picture books (fiction and nonfiction) that are heavy on alliteration. Some excellent ones:

DePaola, Tomie. *Charlie Needs a Cloak.* New York: Simon and Shuster, 1973.

Dragonwagon, Crescent. *All the Awake Animals Are Almost Asleep.* New York: Little, Brown Books, 2012.

Fletcher, Ralph. *Twilight Comes Twice.* New York: Houghton Mifflin Co., 1997.

Moore, Eva. *Lucky Ducklings.* New York: Orchard Books, 2013.

Smith, Maggie. *Pigs in Pajamas.* New York: Alfred A. Knopf, 2012.

Steig, William. *The Toy Brother.* New York: HarperCollins, 1996.

In kindergarten and first grade, as a starting component to daily writing workshop, have children take turns saying words that start with the same letter sound as their name. For fun, make up alliterative names for dolls and stuffed animals in the room: Snoopy Snake, Tiny Teddy Bear, Billy Bird.

Models from Books (grades 1–4)

Go through any of the listed Capstone mentor texts you find in your school and locate the examples of alliteration. Read several of the books to your students, using books you have previously shared with your class for their science content. Reread them specifically to show students the alliteration authors used. Young writers need to learn that when authors write about what they know—expository—they use some of the same techniques they use in story writing.

Other models (grades 2–4)

Have children find examples of alliteration in their independent reading and make a class chart of them. Have students place their initials next to the ones they find and contribute to the chart. Children will find that many books have alliterative titles. Older students will find alliteration in newspaper headlines. They can create lists of them to publish for their writer's notebooks or create collages of the headlines.

Trucks can travel near Deer Creek

Emigres fearful for future of homeland

Farmer exodus in Rwanda stirs fears of starvation

Replica of Nina sails sea of controversy

This sixteen extra sweet

Try It Out Orally (grades K–4)

- Say couplets of alliterative words for your students. For example, *cute cat, Mrs. Moore, red ribbon, bubbling brook, trucks travel.* Tongue twisters are alliteration at work. *Peter Piper picked a peck of pickled peppers.* Rhyming is a variation of alliteration—using the same ending sounds. *A silly cat wore a hat.*

- Have students, looking at photo cards or photographs, create and say phrases that start with the same letters. *Fast fire engine, parked police car, tall teenager, little ladybug.* Invite students to work in partnerships and create two phrases. Conduct a sharing session and build a class chart of their alliterative phrases.

- Find alliterative names among your students. In a class of 30 there is usually one child, and sometimes more, with an alliterative first and last name, or first and middle name: *Melanie Moran, Cory Collins.*

Try It Out in Writing (grades 2–4)

- Model alliteration in its most simple form, making up names for people or animals in your modeled writing: *Big Bear likes to eat blackberries. He roams around looking for fresh food.* Or *Mike Miller is a careful carpenter. He drives a Toyota truck.* Invite students to write several sentences about a person, trying out alliterative names as they do so.

- Model alliteration in descriptive writing using pictures. Have students do the same.

The cat caught a mouse. It's dangling from his mouth.

A pond is a perfect place for a frog. They can sit on little lily pads.

Is your favorite food fish or chicken? Fish is flaky and chicken is chewy. I like both.

- Alliteration in imperative sentences is a common "trick" children's authors use to good effect. Authors use a short pattern consisting of *verb-article-noun*, as in *Mind the moose. Catch a cat. Plant the peas. Dig a ditch.* Have children, in partnerships or groups, construct a similar list. Use the class chart of verbs from your strong-verb lessons as a starting point.

Application and Assessment (grades 2–4)

- Assign *alliteration* as a Target Skill in homework writing journals.
- Teach a lesson about titles, introducing the alliterative title as one technique the pros use. Take a field trip to the school library for children to find alliterative titles in both the fiction and nonfiction sections. Some examples a fourth grade class found:

  Aster Aardvark's Alphabet Adventures by Steven Kellogg

  It Figures!: Fun Figures of Speech by Marvin Terban

  A Medal for Murphy by Melissa W. Odom

  The Tale of Mrs. Tittlemouse by Beatrix Potter

  Tasso of Tarpon Springs by Maity Schrecengost

  Twilight Comes Twice by Ralph Fletcher

- Make *alliteration* a Target Skill in the next piece of writing. After ample student practice, make it a component of the evaluation rubric.

D. Sentence Variation (grades 1–4)

When a piece of writing consists of sentences all the same length and form, readers may get bored or at least become aware of the sameness. They may abandon the text out of boredom.

Author Gary Provost, in his classic writer's guide, *100 Ways to Improve Your Writing*[2], shows why we need to vary our sentence length and form. He writes,

> "Here are five more words. Five-word sentences are fine. But several together become monotonous. Listen to what is happening. The writing is getting boring. The sound of it drones. It's like a stuck record."

[2]Provost, Gary. *100 Ways to Improve Your Writing.* NY: New American Library, 1985. p. 60.

One remedy for boring text rhythm is expanding sentences by adding details that answer one or more of the following questions: **where, when, how,** and **why.**

Whenever you do shared writing with your students, or modeled writing for your students, be sure to write with varying sentence lengths. Vary the form as well, by placing phrases at the start of sentences. *When spring comes,* birds build their nests. *Across the river,* you will find a small farm.

Expanding Sentences

First and second grade teachers tell me that some of their students seem to imitate guided reading or basal texts when they write. *I have a dog. The dog is big. I love big dogs.*

Besides modeling sentences of varying length and form, we need to show these children texts that use a variety of sentence syntax. The mentor text, *I Can Help,* has multiple examples of the simplest expansion of a sentence to tell **where:** *in my city, in my school, in my classroom, in my yard.* **Built from Stone,** illustrates expansion that tells *where, when* and *why.* (All around the world, in New York, in buildings like libraries and museums, since 1798, for years and years, so the gray stone was…, to build their most important buildings, to make smaller pieces.)

Children naturally talk in complex sentences with varied syntax. We want their writing to mimic their normal speech. That is why talking is such an important prewriting activity in the writing process. Providing good models is one of the most effective ways to help children write with varied sentence structures.

Maps

A map is a drawing. It is a drawing of places from a bird's eye view (*where*). A map shows you the location of places with different symbols (*how*). A map can help you find places when you are on a trip or if you are lost (*when*).

Marcia Freeman

Capstone mentor texts that illustrate *varied sentence length:*

Where

> All about Snakes and Lizards
> Built from Stone
> Coral Reefs: Colorful Underwater Habitats (SRT)
> Electricity All Around
> I Can Help
> Let's Rock: Metamorphic Rocks
> Look Inside a Tree
> Rain (Weather Basics) (SRT)
> Tundras
> Which Seed Is This? (SRT)

When

> Built from Stone
> Look Inside a Tree
> Polar Animal Adaptations (SRT)
> Then and Now
> Tundras
> Welcome to North America
> Which Seed Is This? (SRT)

How

> Coral Reefs: Colorful Underwater Habitats (SRT)
> Let's Rock: Metamorphic Rocks
> Look and Learn
> Look Inside a Tree
> The Bloody, Rotten Roman Empire
> Tundras
> Welcome to North America
> Which Seed Is This? (SRT)

Why

> All about Snakes and Lizards
> Animal Spikes and Spines (SRT)
> Animals in Danger in South America
> Built from Stone
> Coral Reefs: Colorful Underwater Habitats (SRT)
> First Nations of North America:
>   Northeast Indians
> Food from Farms (SRT)
> Look Inside a Tree
> Polar Animal Adaptations (SRT)
> The Bloody, Rotten Roman Empire
> Welcome to North America

Introduce the Concept (Awareness) (grades 1–4)

Find a basal-reader text or guided-reading book about the same topic as one of the suggested mentor texts. Since many guided-reading series are built to conform with Common Core State Standards, as are the mentor texts cited in this book, you should be able to find a pair easily.

Read the simple, guided-reading or basal text to your students. Then read the Shared Reading Text. Help students identify the differences in sentence length and how much information the sentences carry. Counting the number of words per sentence is a technique writers use to study their sentence patterns.

Prepare a few sentence strips from each text to show your students graphically how the sentences differ. Help them identify what kind of information the longer sentences contain, that is, *when, where, how, why.*

Discuss with your students which sentences convey more information, i.e., which ones help them to better picture what the author is talking about.

Models from Books (grades 1–4)

Help your students look for other examples of sentences that tell *where, when, how,* and *why* in any of their reading material.

Make four charts, titled **Where, When, How, Why.** As you and the children find examples in text that provides the extra information, add them to the charts. (As always, put children's initials beside their contributions.)

Sample chart entries:

Where: *inside* the flower, *in* the pond, *under* the tree, *out* in space, ...

When: *Early in the summer, in the fall, all year long, when it rains ...*

How: *with its trunk, by hand ...*

Why: *to climb trees, to grip the slippery ice, to grow strong ...*

The chart texts can be reproduced for second, third, and fourth graders to keep in their notebooks for a reference when they are writing independently.

A Comparison of Basal and Capstone Mentor Texts

Simple Text	Capstone Mentor Text: *Welcome to North America*
Canada was formed in 1867.	In 1867, people from northern regions of North America joined together to become one nation called Canada. **(when)**
Mexico has beaches.	People from all around the world travel to Mexico to enjoy its warm sandy beaches. **(why, where)**
The north is cold and the south is hot.	This huge land area is freezing cold in the north, and warm and tropical in the south. **(where)**
People celebrate Cinco de Mayo.	Today people dance, sing, and eat traditional foods on Cinco de Mayo. **(how)**

Try It Out Orally (grades 1–4)

Using photo cards or magazine pictures, provide the opportunity for your students to talk about the photographs, saying both basic sentences and sentences that have been expanded by telling *when, where, how, why.* Model the task for them. Prepare these sentence models using mentor texts beforehand. Display them as sentence strips or write them on an overhead projector. Some examples:

- *First Nations of North America: Northeast Indians,* picture of a water drum used for storytelling/music: *Storytelling was an important way for early Northeast Indians to celebrate their culture and their way of life. (why)*

- *The Bloody, Rotten Roman Empire,* picture of Roman men bathing in bathhouse. Romans did not have soap. Instead, they rubbed themselves with olive oil. Then they scraped themselves clean with a curved metal tool. The oil helped remove the dirt. *(how and why)*

- *Let's Rock: Metamorphic Rocks,* picture of a slate roof: These traditional houses in Nepal have roofs made from slate, a metamorphic rock, split into thin sheets. *(where and how)*

- *Coral Reefs: Colorful Underwater Habitats (SRT),* picture of the polyps: As they die, other polyps build right on top of the empty skeletons. The skeletons pile up to form a reef. It can take hundreds or even thousands of years for the skeletons to form a reef. *(how, where, why)*

In a large group activity have students tell about their pictures. Invite them to try either a basic or an expanded sentence—their classmates can tell which one it is.

Model this as a partner or group activity. Have older students work in groups to create sentences that contain more than one of the phrases. Example: *In the fall, many small animals make their homes under a tree so they don't get cold.* Don't expect the sentences to be graceful. Let your young writers have fun with this exercise in language development.

Try It Out in Writing (grades 1–4)

In shared writing, construct a paragraph about a Shared Reading Text cover. Invite children to supply the sentences and emphasize the use of phrases that give extra information about *where, when, how,* and *why.* Write sentences without the phrases if they are articulated as such. Skip lines and after the paragraph is finished, show your young writers where they can revise by adding phrases with a caret (^).

Invite children to try this out in their writing to a picture or any independent writing they do during writing workshop.

Establish these phrases as the Target Skill for the week or for a genre piece that older students work on independently.

Revision Model

Model getting rid of short Dinky Sentences by having third and fourth graders count the words per sentence in practice pieces they wrote weeks earlier. When several young writers find short sentences that give very little information, invite them to the board to write their examples. Show them how to expand Dinky Sentences by adding *when, where, how,* and *why* phrases. Have them, with a partner they select as a consultant, revise their sentences at the board. (See Practice and Application in Describing with Verbs, at the start of this chapter for other cases of Dinky Sentences.)

Practice and Application (grades 1–4)

- Provide opportunities for your young writers to practice this expanded-sentence skill in short paragraphs related to their science, social studies, art, and math work. For example, after a science activity involving electricity and batteries, and having shared the mentor text, ***Electricity All Around,*** have students construct a list of all the battery usage they experience in their life. Have them write one- to three-sentence paragraphs about two to three of the uses with which they are the most familiar. A Target Skill for their writing will be to expand their sentences with phrases that tell the reader *where, when, why, how:*

Flashlight...on a summer night.   **(when)**

CD player...to play my favorite songs.   **(where)**

Cordless drill...on our tree house floor. **(where)**

- Place two or three *related* Dinky Sentences (a short paragraph) on the board each morning for students to expand using the functions of *where, when, how,* or *why* as well as editing for writing conventions.

- Assign *sentence expansion* as a Target Skill in homework journaling, in writing center, and in independent writing.

Assessment (grades 2–4)

Take note of your students' abilities to expand sentences. Use their practice writing to diagnose for review or remedial lessons about the skill. Assess their uses of the skill in an assigned piece only after ample practice. Place representative writing in students' portfolios for proof of progress and to use in parent conferencing.

Chapter 4: **Beginnings and Endings**

Composing the first sentence of a piece is tough. How do we capture our reader's attention? And, composing an ending is harder still. How do we sum things up and exit gracefully? These are two puzzles that writers of all ages have to solve.

Whether young writers jump right into their informational expository pieces as kindergarten and first graders do or use organization schemes as older students do, they can all learn how to begin and end their pieces in graceful ways that satisfy their readers. Here are some simple lessons, using Capstone mentor texts as models, that you can use to help your young writers begin and end their pieces like the pros.

Lessons

A. Beginnings (grades K–4)

The first sentence or two of a piece must let the reader know what it is about. You, the author, having written the body of your piece, know where you want to lead your readers.

What you have to figure out is how best to get their attention so they will follow you there.

The first sentence is called the **hook** or lead. Whatever form it takes, it should intrigue, invite, and raise a reader's curiosity. It can be written in many forms—question, exclamation, sentence fragments, riddle, talking directly to the reader, a quote, a definition, words in bold font, sounds, etc.—that help it achieve its goal.

Capstone mentor texts that illustrate *beginning techniques young writers can emulate:*

Question
  Animal Migration
  Countries Around the World: Czech Republic
  Countries Around the World: Scotland
  First Nations of North America: Great Basin Indians
  Fun at the Zoo
  Goliath Bird-Eating Spiders and Other Extreme Bugs
  Oceans
  Storm Tracker: Measuring and Forecasting
  The Dreadful, Smelly Colonies
  The Environment Challenge: Bridging the Energy Gap (Express Edition)
  The Terrible, Awful Civil War
  Weather Watchers: Weather (SRT)

Exclamation
  Fun at the Zoo
  Giraffes (SRT)
  Polar Animal Adaptations (SRT)
  The Bloody, Rotten Roman Empire
  Tundras
  Welcome to Mexico

Talking Directly to the Reader
  A Monarch Butterfly's Journey
  Animals in Danger in South America
  Animals with No Eyes
  Coral Reefs: Colorful Underwater Habitats (SRT)
  Countries Around the World: Chile
  Countries Around the World: Czech Republic
  Meat-Eating Plants and Other Extreme Plant Life
  Monsters of the Deep
  Rain Forests: Gardens of Green (SRT)
  The Attractive Truth about Magnetism
  The Bloody, Rotten Roman Empire
  The Dreadful, Smelly Colonies
  The Terrible, Awful Civil War

Definition
  Community Helpers
  Crystals
  Deserts
  Grasslands
  Oceans
  The Environment Challenge: Bridging the Energy
      Gap (Express Edition)
  The Life Cycle of Birds
  The U.S. Supreme Court (American Symbols)
  Welcome to Mexico
  Which Seed Is This? (SRT)

Setting
  Ancient Greece: Birthplace of Democracy
  Animals with No Eyes
  Lightning
  Monsters of the Deep
  Scaly Blood Squirters and Other
      Extreme Reptiles
  The Bloody, Rotten Roman Empire
  The U.S. Constitution, Bill of Rights,
      and a New Nation
  What Did the Aztecs Do for Me?
  What Did the Vikings Do for Me?

Onomatopoeia
  If I Were a Veterinarian
  Meat-Eating Plants and Other Extreme Plant Life
  Polar Animal Adaptations (SRT)
  The Crude, Unpleasant Age of Pirates
  Water: Up, Down, and All Around

Introduce the Concept (Awareness) (grades K–4)

Gather your students at the start of a daily writing workshop and talk to them about the writing process. Ask them what they like about writing and the things they do as writers. Review some lessons they have studied, such as strong verbs (what's happening), using color and number words, etc.

Tell them that when you yourself write, you are often puzzled about the first thing to say to your readers. "I want them to read my work, so how do I get their attention? Should I say, 'Hey, read my piece.' Or, 'Hi, my name is Marcy and I am going to tell you about fire engines.'? Let's look at what the pros do." Gather several mentor texts that the students and you have shared previously.

• In **kindergarten and first grade** use the books that start with a question hook. Open each book and read the first lines. Show the children the text and point to the punctuation. "The writer asks the reader a question. I bet we could do that!" Introduce Exclamation hooks after Question hooks. (Every piece of writing does not need a hook at this grade level. But, encourage your students to think about what will get their reader's attention and what will make the reader want to read their piece.)

• In **second through fourth grade** introduce a full variety of hook devices. Start with a question, an exclamation, and onomatopoeia, and continue with the rest of the devices illustrated by the mentor texts. The hooks you introduce will depend on your students' prior knowledge of the concept and the hook types they already use. The list of devices in this lesson is not exhaustive, but it is a place to start in elementary grades.

Try It Out Orally (grades K–4)

1. Midyear Kindergarten and First Grade

Knowing the cue words for questions *(who, what, when, where, why, how, which one)* and the inverted verb form *(is it, was it, did you, etc.)* as well as making the sound of a question with a voice rise in pitch are typical primary skills. Therefore, the question hook is a good choice for introducing young writers to the concept of beginnings.

Gather your students to the class meeting place and use a mentor text cover or photograph to model, orally, how to ask a question about the photo. Display a class chart with the words *Who, What, When, Where, How,* and *Why.* Model how to ask a question using one of the cue words.

Invite your students to ask questions about the photo. Have young writers give each other the silent *thumbs-up* signal for good writing (talking) when they successfully ask a question. Display other pictures and continue this exercise.

Invite your students to select photos from the class set or to draw one of their own during the writing component of writing workshop. Invite them to ask questions as they talk to their writing partners or you, as you rove and encourage, take dictation, or meet with them for guided writing.

Shared Writing

On the following day, do shared writing with the children, scribing as they compose a piece either about a picture or a shared experience. Encourage them to start the class piece with a question. They may compose the piece without a hook. If so, leave room at the top to write the hook after they have finished the piece. (Adding the hook later is a good opportunity to model revision.)

2. Second through Fourth Grade

Prepare a series of short paragraphs lacking a hook to project on an overhead or to reproduce for each student. Gather the class and review the type of hook they have been studying. After you have shown them Capstone mentor texts that use that hook, ask them to form partnerships and create hooks of that type for the text you display or give to them. Stress that this is oral work only. (Use these models for a written exercise later.)

Question Hook Engenders Answer

When primary students first use a question for the hook, they most often follow it with the answer. As long as they elaborate, do not be concerned about this.

IN PROGRESS

Mike   9/30

T.S.
periods
? hook

What is it? is it a bird nest?

Mabby it is a Bird Haows fam The

East a 1000 miyls away fom hery.

A first grader practices a question hook.

If the hook device you are teaching is onomatopoeia, the paragraph you prepare should be about something with which students can associate a sound. A paragraph about popcorn, a beach, farm, city streets, airport, or firehouse would lend itself to using onomatopoeia as a hook. If you are introducing definition as a hook device, the paragraph should describe an object, game, sport, or process that students can define. Two samples are included here for your use.

Onomatopoeia

_____ .

Nothing quite sounds like the zoo at feeding time. The chimps fling themselves around their cages when they smell the fruit their keepers bring.

The seals set up a chorus as they see the buckets of fish their keepers carry. You'd better take a set of earplugs the next time you visit the zoo at dinner hour.

(Beginning sounds your students might compose are Eeeeee, eeeee, eeee. Arrrrrfffff, arrrrffff. Remember, there are no correct spellings for made-up sound words.)

Definition

_____ .

The ball is a bit bigger, about the size of a grapefruit. You use a bat and the rules are similar. It's perfect for a picnic event when you have all-sized kids and grown-ups because most of them can't hit the ball as far or fast as they could if it were a baseball.

(Beginning definitions your students might compose: _Softball is a safe ball game. Softball is a lot like baseball._ Or _Softball is a game like baseball._)

After the students have worked together, hold a sharing session and chart their hook creations. Be sure to enter the initials of the contributors.

Other Models (grades 1–4)

- Call attention to the hooks under study whenever you read aloud to your class. Besides the Capstone mentor texts, _Ranger Rick_ magazine and nonfiction picture books abound with these devices.

- Show students writing samples from other young writers who used hooks under study.

- Take your students to the school library to collect first sentences and hooks from magazine articles and informational books. Have them write the sentences on strips of paper. On returning to the classroom, help the children sort and classify the hooks. Make a class chart of all the kinds they found. Publish the list for second, third, and fourth graders to put in their writer's notebooks.

- Ask older students to bring in examples they find in their independent reading and add them to a class chart: Hooks Under Study.

Try It Out in Writing (grades 1–4)

- Model *question hooks* in writing for your students, using a picture as a prompt. For example, writing about a picture of a police horse, start with *Have you ever seen a police horse up close?* rather than *Hi, my name is Joe, I am going to tell you three things about police horses.* (A definite *thumbs-down!*)

- In later lessons, model *Exclamations* and *Onomatopoeia* for hooks. *Watch out! That garbage truck is backing up.* Or, *Pop, Pop, Pop. My mom makes popcorn for everyone when we watch TV.*

- Use the prepared samples for definition and onomatopoeia hooks in a writing exercise. Conversely, have your students write similar short paragraphs to trade with partners, each writing an appropriate hook.

Young writers' initial imitations may not be as catchy as a published book or *Ranger Rick* magazine author's, but the technique is the same. And as students become more facile with the skill, they will become more creative.

Practice and Application (grades 1–4)

Invite students to use the *hook* under study as a Target Skill in their independent writing. Post the skill in a writing center. Call for its use in homework writing journals.

Have your young writers meet in peer conferences over their practice writing and award each other stickers for hitting the hook Target Skill. Model these kinds of peer conferences for your students often.

Diagnose/Assess (grades 1–4)

Keep anecdotal records of your young writers' uses of the different hook types you teach them. Read their practice pieces and journal entries to see if they understand the skill. After ample practice, call for an independent piece and let them know that you will be assessing it for the hook and the other targets under study. You might administer prompted pieces (use pictures with youngest students) on a periodic schedule to assess current skills. Always provide students with the scoring rubric (criteria) for the prompted piece so they will know what is expected of them.

In grades three and four, you might create writing-craft quizzes to assess your students' knowledge. A sample item might be: Name three hook devices authors use in expository writing. Or: For the following paragraph (a short, easy-to-read paragraph with writing space preceding it) write a hook that gets your reader's attention and lets him know what the paragraph will be about.

B. Endings (grades 1–4)

Writers, young and old, often find that endings are the hardest part of composing a piece. Many children will simply stop when they get to the end of a page. To them the end is a physical entity. If you tell them, "You don't have an ending," they will point to the bottom of the page and say, "There's the end." If you still don't get it, they will help you out by writing, in large capital letters at the bottom of their work, THE END.

While students in grades K–3 should not be expected to write ending *paragraphs,* they nevertheless can end their pieces in a simple and satisfying manner, consisting of a sentence or two.

Besides telling how they feel about the subject, professional and student writers use a variety of ending devices. Capstone book authors demonstrate the following:

- using a universal word
- asking the reader a question
- giving the final step in a process
- exclamations
- circling back to the hook to repeat that device
- summarizing

Capstone mentor texts that illustrate *ending techniques:*

Universal Word

A universal-word ending employs general terms, such as: *always, all, all of us, people the world over, the world, everyone, everywhere, every day, everything, every time, everybody, no one, nobody, etc.* For example: At the end of a piece about roller skating as a favorite activity, a second grader writes *I could go skating every day.*

Bread around the World
Finding Patterns
Grasslands
Lend a Hand
Measure for Measure
Oceans
Our Global Community (SRT)
The Terrible, Awful Civil War
Tundras

Ask the Reader a Question

When authors use this ending device they may ask the same question as the hook or they may modify it to reflect the material covered in the piece. It is a way of asking the reader: What do you remember? What did you learn?

All about Snakes and Lizards
Animals with No Eyes
Community Helpers
Rain Forest Animal Adaptations (SRT)
The Attractive Truth about Magnetism
The Environment Challenge:
  Bridging the Energy Gap (Express Edition)
Using Your Senses (SRT)
Weather Watchers: Weather (SRT)
Welcome to Mexico
You Can Write an Amazing Journal

The Final Step in a Sequence

In a piece organized in step-sequence, writers often use numbers, letters, or transition words, such as: *first, second, next, after that, …* When they reach the last step they signal it with words, such as: *finally, now, the last thing, lastly, etc.*

A Monarch Butterfly's Journey
Ancient Greece: Birthplace of Democracy
Cooking Pancakes
Mapping
Who Really Created Democracy?
Who Really Discovered America?

Exclamations

Exclamations are used for emphasis or repetition. An ending exclamation often reiterates the title, or beginning as you will find in most of the listed books.

All about Boats
Cooking Pancakes
Fun at the Zoo
Graphs
If I Were the President
If the Shoe Fits
Ocean Animal Adaptations (SRT)
Oranges: From Fruit to Juice
The Bloody, Rotten Roman Empire
The Crude, Unpleasant Age of Pirates
The Dreadful, Smelly Colonies
Then and Now

Circling Back to the Hook

Circling back to the hook means repeating at the end of a piece the form of the beginning technique. For example, if you ask the reader a question as a hook, then ask another related question at the end or repeat the question and give the answer.

A fourth grader began a piece with *Reading takes you places you'd never go,* and then commenced to write about her love of books. She ended with *Reading brings you friends you'd never know,* repeating the form of the hook and creating a rhyme. Very nice.

Desert Animal Adaptations
If the Shoe Fits
Inventions
Look and Learn
The Crude, Unpleasant Age of Pirates
Who Really Created Democracy?
Who Really Discovered America?

Summarizing

Sometimes authors like to review the main ideas in a piece, so they list the most important things they want their readers to remember. The ending may be in the form of a reminder, a question, an imperative statement, a prediction, etc. *Ponds are great places to spot animals. Sit and watch them, but remember: Even shallow water can be dangerous… Do not remove plants or animals from ponds…* (from **Look Inside a Pond**).

Coral Reefs: Colorful Underwater Habitats (SRT)
Look Inside a Pond
Polar Animal Adaptations (SRT)
Science Tools
The Crude, Unpleasant Age of Pirates
The Lincoln Memorial (American Symbols)
The Story of Corn
The Terrible, Awful Civil War
The U.S. Constitution, Bill of Rights,
  and a New Nation
Which Seed Is This? (SRT)

Introduce the Concept (Awareness) (grades 1–4)

Gather your students at the start of the daily writing workshop to talk to them about the writing process. Tell them that the ending of a piece is just as important as the beginning. Just as writers use hook devices, they use ending devices.

Show them some student samples of writing that end abruptly with *The End*. Then show them student samples in which young writers ask their readers a question or use an exclamation or a universal word.

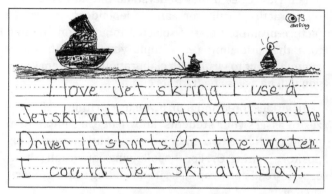

A second grader uses the universal word ending.

A fourth grader practices several craft techniques including a universal word ending.

If you have not collected samples, construct sample texts of your own. Show your students that you practice Target Skills too.

Suggest to your first through fourth graders that they look at what the pros do to end their writing. *Let's look at what Capstone authors do.* Gather several mentor texts that the students have shared with you previously. Read the last page or two and discuss the various endings the authors used.

Try It Out Orally (grades 1–4)

- In the primary grades, prepare short, informative text models that contain a *question* ending. Read them to your students. Stop before you get to the ending and ask them to provide an ending of their own. Then show them what the author, you, did.

Your short text example might be: Using the cover of **Using Your Senses,** a collage of photos of the tongue, eyes, ears, fingers, and nose:

Five Senses

We learn all about the world seeing and hearing. We can also smell, feel, and taste things. I learned not to put my hand on the stove when I was four. I learned not to eat paste when I was in kindergarten and tried it. What have you learned with your five senses?

- In grades two and higher, do the same exercises, creating or selecting text that illustrates the ending devices under study. Have students think of and say endings of their own. On another occasion, provide sample texts with no endings for them to read on their own. Again, have them contribute endings that use the device under study.

Models from Mentor Texts (grades 2–4)

Collect and sort endings: Gather a large selection of photo-illustrated informational texts, either in Shared Reading Text form or student copies, or take your students on a writing field trip to the school library. Have them collect samples of ending sentences from the Shared Reading Texts or other nonfiction photo-illustrated books or magazines for primary children. Just as you did with hook techniques, help them sort and classify them according to the endings they know or are studying (see page 69). Make a class chart and publish the list for their writing notebooks.

Try It Out in Writing (grades K–4)

- In a shared writing starting component to your class daily writing workshop, help your students write a small composition about an agreed upon subject. Draw the bull's-eye archery target in the upper right-hand corner and write, *Target Skill: Ending.* Remind them they are to practice one of the endings under study.

- During the independent writing component of daily writing workshop, have second, third, and fourth graders practice endings on short pieces, a paragraph or two of writing. They can use picture prompts or write about a topic from their personal expertise lists. Assign only the one Target Skill: an ending device. When they are finished they should meet in peer conferences and identify the type of endings used, awarding each other with stickers or highlighting the ending on each manuscript. Call a sharing session to hear the endings created. This writing should not be assessed.

A Creative Ending

In a third grade class where I worked with young writers, a student wrote about a picture featuring cheetahs, his favorite animal. He selected one of the ending categories his class had found from their library research—**Invite your reader to learn more**—and ended his piece with: *For more information call 1-800-CHEETAH.* He was copying the pros, using a technique he saw on television. That idea swept the community of writers and for a while everyone's piece ended with, Call 1-800-topic. Everyone loved this new technique and added it to their bank of knowledge of the writing craft.

Practice and Application (grades 2–4)

Invite students to use the *ending device* under study as a Target Skill in their independent writing. Post the skill in a writing center. Call for its use in homework writing journals.

Have your young writers meet in peer conferences to hear independent and journal writing and award each other stickers for hitting the Target Skill. Make it a practice to have young authors call their classmates' attention to good examples they hear in peer conferences.

Diagnose/Assess (grades 1–4)

Keep anecdotal records of your young writers' uses of *ending techniques.* Read their practice pieces and journal entries to see if they understand the skill. After ample practice, call for an independent piece (a picture-prompted or self-selected topic, or one related to a thematic unit; i.e., a topic your students know enough about to write with elaboration). Let them know you will be assessing it for its ending.

In grades three and four, if you use writing-craft quizzes to assess your students' knowledge, a sample item might be: Name two ending devices authors use in expository writing. Or: For the following paragraph (short, easy-to-read paragraph), write an ending using a *universal word.*

Teach your young writers these simple beginning and ending techniques. Model them through your own writing. Point them out in literature. Encourage your students to imitate the pros. Watch them grow as writers.

Chapter 5: **Preparing Students for Comprehensive Assessment Tests**

More and more states are implementing comprehensive assessment tools. These performance-based tests require students to analyze and interpret illustrated narrative or informational text and write responses of a sentence or a paragraph. The illustrations may be artistic drawings or graphic representations of information in the form of captioned or labeled photographs, diagrams, charts, tables, graphs, and maps. Students must refer to both the source text and graphics to find supporting details for their responses.

We can begin as early as the primary grades to prepare students for such tasks; not only for success on comprehensive tests but for continuing success in performing similar tasks associated with their academic studies and their jobs.

We start by teaching our young writers how to

- interpret pictures as a precursor to interpreting text, i.e., making inferences and finding evidence in the form of descriptive details to support those inferences,
- identify specific kinds of supporting details to help interpret text,
- use supporting details in their own informational writing,
- organize and present information in a variety of graphic forms, and
- interpret graphic information.

The lessons in this chapter will show you how to use Capstone mentor texts and photographs to support this instruction.

Lessons

You should present these lessons in the same fashion as the writing-craft lessons described earlier in this book. Follow the How to Teach a Writing Craft Skill described in the How to Use This Book section on page 13. Once you have used this sequence to teach the nonfiction writing lessons, you should be able to apply it to the lessons in this chapter.

A. Supporting Details from Pictures (grades K–4)

1. Interpreting Pictures: "I Think ..." or, "I Can See That ..."

In kindergarten and first grade introduce the phrases *I think* and *I can see that* as Target Skills when children describe their drawings or the pictures on Shared Reading Text covers or photo cards. Orally model this for your class, demonstrate it in shared and modeled writing, and have students practice it both orally and in writing.

For example, using the cover photo of *Healthy Eating*, you might say: *I think the girl likes watermelon. She is smiling and she has already taken a big bite out of the melon.* After students select their pictures, have them tell a partner what they think about their pictures. Prompt them with some of the following questions.

- What can you learn from the picture?
- What do you think the photographer is trying to show you?
- What do you think is happening?
- Why do you think the animal or person is doing that?
- Where do you think this scene, person, or animal is?

- What season or what time of day do you think it is?
  - What is the weather (outside scene)?
  - Do you see anything that has a name?
  - What can you count in the picture?
  - What do you think happened before the picture was taken?
  - What do you predict will happen after the picture was taken?

Many of the children's observations and subsequent *I think* statements cannot or will not be substantiated by evidence in the picture. Do not be concerned; rather, encourage students to talk or write freely about their pictures, telling what they think.

Be ready to accept primary children's answers without correcting them. They have far less experience than you and are very literal. They may not place the same interpretation upon a picture as an adult. The important thing is to encourage them to think and articulate what they think. (Significant vocabulary building occurs when children talk to one another about pictures. Because they are free to choose pictures of subjects that relate to their experience, they usually have the vocabulary to talk about them. In doing so, they teach their peers.)

If your second, third, or fourth graders have not had the opportunity to do this exercise in the primary grades, use it and the subsequent lesson early in the school year. Add *I think* or *I can see that* to their Target Skill list when they are writing descriptively.

2. Interpreting pictures and providing evidence: "I think …" or, "I can see that … because …"

Once children talk or write what they think about a picture, show them that writers support their opinions or statements with facts, or evidence. We can call this *finding the evidence* or *giving supporting details*. Finding the evidence or giving supporting details is comparable to "Oh, yeah? Prove it!," the playground challenge engendered by bragging or dubious claims.

Return to the picture you used to introduce, *I think* and *I can see that*. Show your students the difference between a statement about a photograph that can be proven or supported with evidence and one that cannot.

- ***Mapping Your Community*** cover: *I can see that this is an aerial photograph.* Proof: *I can see rooftops and roads.* No proof: *I think the place is in California.*
- ***Pushes and Pulls*** cover: *I think the girl in the swing is not scared to be pushed.* Proof: *She is smiling. When you are scared you look it.* No proof: *I think the girls are sisters.*
- ***Life in the Time of Abraham Lincoln and the Civil War*** cover: *I think this is a picture taken in the old days.* Proof: *All the men have mustaches and beards and high collars.* No proof: *I think the men are waiting for supper.*

Through **shared** and **modeled writing**, illustrate this *finding of evidence* for statements we make about a picture. Model the use of the phrases *I think*, or *I can tell … because* (evidence). After students are able to articulate similar proofs, ask them to practice this in writing.

B. Supporting Details in Text (grades 1–4)

Fluency is the paramount goal of an elementary school writing program. Fourth and fifth graders should easily be able to write a page or more about a topic commensurate with their knowledge or experience. They should be comfortable with composing and be able to organize and develop their ideas. Fluent writers develop their ideas and extend their information and explanations with supporting details.

I think
I think this person is training this horse to race. This is a race track. I have proof because I see he has a wip, helmet, googls, and when they race they have plad shirts or stripes.

I think
that this kitten is trying to figure out what this stuffed animal is and is very curious. I can tell this because the kitten is putting it's nose to the teddy bear.

I think
This man likes planting
Evidence
Because the rest of his garden looks like it's growing well and has had the proper care.

I think
I think that people or artists are trying to draw a horse because they have an eral and pencial and the horse is in a pose.

Practice   Proof

I think this man in the picture is a farmer. I think this because I see a farm in the bachround. I think that the seasons are turning from winter [spring] to Fall. I have proof because I see a crops are ready to be picked and he's wearing a sweater and jeans. I think he's picked a grain to check and making sure it's ready to be harvest.

Supporting Details

Supporting details are specific and can be named, i.e., made concrete—just right for your young writers. Among the kinds of supporting details that you will find in Capstone mentor texts are:

- **descriptive details:** see Chapter 3, Composing Skills—Description
- **specific examples**
- **definitions**
- **comparisons:** see Chapter 3, Composing Skills—Descriptive Comparisons
- **numbers**
- **reasons why**
- **graphics such as photo-insets, close-ups, diagrams, symbols, and maps**

Authoritative quotes (testimonials) and narrative vignettes (real-life examples) are two other powerful supporting details used by nonfiction writers. I refer you to *Listen to This: Developing an Ear for Expository*, in which you will find a treatment of authoritative quotes, narrative vignettes, and other supporting details applicable to both informational writing and essay.

1. Specific Examples (grades 2–4)

If you can say or write **"For example,"** or **"For instance,"** before an added piece of information, you are giving a specific example. For example, in ***Simply Science: Electricity*** (page 18), the author tells us that *Inventors found many ways to use electrical energy.* Subsequent sentences give specific examples: *motors, lightbulbs, radios, TVs, toasters, vacuum cleaners.*

Specific examples support statements and extend the reader's knowledge and understanding, just as descriptive examples, discussed in Chapter 3, Composing Skills, help readers visualize information. Specific examples can be added to information using the cue words: *such as, like, for example,* or using a dash (—) or no cue word with *For example* implied. Here are some examples from Capstone nonfiction books:

- Many familiar songs today began in other countries. One *such* song is "Yankee Doodle." (***One Land, Many Cultures***)
- No matter where you live, your weather follows patterns. You may get rainy springs, hot summers, cool falls, and snowy winters. (***Warning: Extreme Weather***) *For example* is implied before the second sentence.

- Besides studying rocks, some geologists may choose to study other parts of Earth—soil, mountains, rivers, oceans, and more. (*Rocks and Minerals*)

Specific examples can also be added as graphics: labeled photo-inserts, close-ups, and far views. (See Presenting Information Graphically, which starts on page 79.)

Capstone mentor texts that illustrate the use of a specific example as a supporting detail:

Animals in Danger in South America
Animals with No Eyes
Comparing Materials (SRT)
Coral Reefs: Colorful Underwater Habitats (SRT)
Countries Around the World: England
Countries Around the World: France
Desert Animal Adaptations
First Nations of North America: California Indians
Life Cycles (Watch It Grow) (SRT)
One Land, Many Cultures
Parks of the U.S.A.
Polar Animal Adaptations (SRT)
Rocks and Minerals
Simply Science
The Life Cycle of Birds
Tundras
Warning: Extreme Weather
Weather Watchers: Weather (SRT)

The Word Game: "Such As" (grades 2–3)

Play the following word game "Such As" with your young writers in a whole-class activity. It is a variation of an old playground ball-bouncing game called "A, My Name is Alice." It goes like this, in chant form:

> X (the chanter says the first letter of his or her name), my name is (chanter says his or her first name) and I like (names a category of things such as toys, sports, vegetables, food, cars, books, people, weather) *Such As* (names things in the category that start with the same letters as his or her name).

> **A,** my name is **Alyisha** and I like fruit *Such As* **apples** and **apricots.**

> **B,** my name is **Benji** and I like sports *Such As* **basketball, baseball,** and **biking.**

> **D,** my name is **Daren** and I like food *Such As* **donuts** and **dill pickles.**

> And so on.

Explain the game, model two or three chant lines, then give your students time to create their own chant lines. Encourage them to work in partnerships. Do the chants to tapping or clapping to provide a cadence. Have your students try this out while jumping rope or bouncing a handball on the playground.

Specific Examples as a Target Skill (grades 2–4)

In **peer conferences,** have your young writers ask each other for *Specific Examples* when they listen to each other's independent writing or writing from science, social studies, and math.

Model how to revise sentences by adding information in the form of specific examples. Using primary-level informational texts, show students how to add specific examples when none are given. Children love to revise book text—they say, "See, the author should have done what we do!" When they are encouraged to look in professional text for the same Target Skills they are studying and using, they become very critical readers.

Do this orally first. Use a primary Shared Reading Text and have students look for text that can be extended with specific examples. For example, using *Soil,* turn to page 4, and read the last sentence: *There are many animals living in the soil, too!* Ask children what specific examples of animals live in the soil. After they offer a few examples, model for them how to add the specific examples to the sentence thusly: *There are many animals living in the soil, such as worms, mice, moles, and insects.*

2. Definitions (grades 3–4)

Nonfiction writers must define new, topic-related words or phrases for their readers. Capstone mentor texts use vocabulary particular to the content topic. The vocabulary of science, math, geography, or history is as specific and specialized as the vocabulary of musicians, artists, carpenters, plumbers, computer scientists, astronauts, electricians, doctors, mechanics, bankers, writers, you-name-it. Sharing a specialized vocabulary makes it easier for specialists to communicate. Listen to two mechanics or two violinists talking about their specialties. If you are mechanically or musically challenged, you probably do not understand much of what they say.

When specialists write to explain or inform nonspecialists, they must define the terms they use. Young writers can learn to present definitions in several ways, using mentor text examples.

- You can define something in dictionary style: *Tortillas are a kind of flat, round Mexican bread.* **(Welcome to Mexico)**

- You can define something by saying what it is made of: *Pirates ate a steady diet of hardtack. Made of flour and water, these hard biscuits didn't spoil as quickly as meat.* **(The Crude, Unpleasant Age of Pirates)**

- You can define it by telling what it does: *They gathered eggs from wild birds and hunted ducks with weapons called bolas. The weapon is thrown through the air to hit and kill birds.* **(First Nations of North America: Arctic Peoples)**

- You can define something by calling it by another name, usually set off by commas or using the word *or:*
  - *Some snakes have long teeth called fangs.* **(Animal Spikes and Spines)**
  - *That's why concrete is used to make the base, or foundation, of a new building.* **(Built from Stone)**
  - *The natural chemicals that occur in food are called nutrients.* **(Food Technology)**

Capstone nonfiction mentor texts that illustrate *definition as a supporting detail:*

Animal Spikes and Spines (SRT)
Animals with No Eyes
Built from Stone
Coral Reefs: Colorful Underwater Habitats (SRT)
First Nations of North America: Arctic Peoples
First Nations of North America: Northeast Indians
Food Technology
Fun at the Zoo
Goliath Bird-Eating Spiders and Other Extreme Bugs
If the Shoe Fits
Life Cycles (Watch It Grow) (SRT)
Meat-Eating Plants and other Extreme Plant Life
Oceans
Polar Animal Adaptations (SRT)
Soil
The Crude, Unpleasant Age of Pirates

The Environment Challenge: Bridging the Energy Gap (Express Edition)
Weather Watchers: Weather (SRT)
Welcome to Mexico
What Is a Family? (SRT)

Definition as a Target Skill

Definition can be introduced as a revision Target Skill in third grade and higher when students write about math, science, social studies, art, and music. Whenever students use vocabulary specific to the topic, they have opportunities to add definitions. Model how to do this as a revision process.

Sample text: *The playground is filled with geometric shapes. The slide, its ladder, and the ground make a triangle. The climbing bar rungs form squares.*

Revision through definition: *The playground is filled with geometric shapes,* (define) *closed figures made up of straight or curved lines. The slide, its ladder, and the ground make a triangle,* (define) *a shape with three straight sides and three angles. The climbing bar rungs form squares* (define)—*every one of the four straight sides is the same length.*

3. Numbers (grades 1–4)

Numbers quantify information, making it concrete and more factual, real, and believable. Numbers constitute a form of evidence or supporting detail.

Using photo cards or other picture sources, model the use of numbers in shared and modeled writing. Ask students to include numbers in their descriptive writing. Make number use a Target Skill in writing centers and during independent writing.

To Spell a Number or Not

You will need to review two rules about writing numbers with your students. They are called the Rule of 9 and the Rule of 99. In **nonfiction** writing, the numbers zero to nine are usually presented in spelled-out form. Larger numbers are presented in numerical form: 25, 102. In **fiction,** numbers from one to 99 are spelled out. And, if a character says a number in dialogue, spell it out no matter how large it is—people speak in words, not numerals.

According to The Mentor Guide to Punctuation,[1] "Regardless of subject and field, more and more editors, writers, and publishers are choosing numerals over spelled-out numbers. These reasons may be given: Readers grasp numerals more quickly than spelled-out numbers, and numerals are easier and faster to write than awkward, long combinations of spelled-out numbers. In addition, as we become more and more of a computer-oriented society, we will probably become a more and more numeral-oriented society."

[1]*The Mentor Guide to Punctuation*, by William C. Paxson, New American Library, NY, 1986. p. 131.

> Practice
>
> 1 2 3 4 5 6   T.
>
> Do you want to go fishing? Come with fisherman Fred, the greatest fisher on the face of Earth. He just caught a 59 pound Salmon in Lake Okachobe. Fred used a 15 pound test, and a chunk of mino. Doesn't he look happy? Also that day he caught 5 more salmon too. Didn't he have a fantastic day? You could too if you go to Lake Okachobe.

Capstone nonfiction mentor texts that illustrate *the use of a number as a supporting detail:*

Ancient Greece: Birthplace of Democracy
Animals with No Eyes
Coral Reefs: Colorful Underwater Habitats (SRT)
Countries Around the World: England
Countries Around the World: France
First Nations of North America: California Indians
First Nations of North America:
   Great Basin Indians
From Egg to Snake
From Mealworm to Beetle (SRT)
Let's Rock: Metamorphic Rocks
Look Inside a Tree
Parks of the U.S.A.
Polar Animal Adaptations (SRT)
The Lincoln Memorial (American Symbols)
Which Seed Is This? (SRT)

4. Reasons Why (grades 2–4)

Writers use *reasons why* to explain their information further. They may present this supporting detail as a phrase, a sentence, or several sentences, which may be preceded by cue words or a comma. For example:

- **to,** from the implied phrase, **in order to:** Workers use machines <u>to</u> remove the skins, to take out the pits, and <u>to</u> dice the fruit.
- **for:** People used shells and beads <u>for</u> money.
- **because:** What goes up must come down. This is <u>because</u> of gravity.
- **so that:** Subways were constructed <u>so that</u> surface transportation did not become a gridlock.
- **a comma:** Cattle egrets follow the herd, increasing their opportunity for insect food.
- **no cue word or comma:** Taking care of a garden is a lot of work. <u>You have to weed, plant, water, and harvest.</u>

Capstone nonfiction mentor texts that illustrate *the reason why as a supporting detail:*

Animals in Danger in South America
Animal Spikes and Spines (SRT)
Coral Reefs: Colorful Underwater Habitats (SRT)
Goliath Bird-Eating Spiders and Other
   Extreme Bugs
Look Inside a Tree
Meat-Eating Plants and Other Extreme Plant Life
The Crude, Unpleasant Age of Pirates
The Environment Challenge: Bridging the
   Energy Gap (Express Edition)
The Life Cycle of Birds
Welcome to Mexico
Which Seed Is This? (SRT)

Return to Chapter 3, Composing Skills—Expanding Sentences, for more activities associated with this Target Skill.

5. Named Examples (Specificity) (grades 1–4)

One of the joys of reading is recognizing the familiar—being able to say, *That is just like me; I do that, too; I've been there.* When an author writes, *The granite used in this monument comes from Vermont,* all of us Vermonters smile. When an author writes, *These animals like to eat ants—doodlebugs, anteaters, woodpeckers,* everyone who has kept a doodlebug as a pet smiles at that sentence.

It is an author's job to give his readers that joy. **Specificity** is the means for doing it. Instead of writing *store,* write *hardware store.* Instead of writing *game,* write *Scrabble.* Instead of writing *cereal,* write *Fruit Loops.* A specific noun conveys more meaning, more imagery. The text comes alive and engages the reader.

Specificity is not just a technique for engaging readers and making them smile. It has the most important function of establishing concrete examples and evidence to support information and ideas.

Capstone nonfiction mentor texts that illustrate *the use of specificity, using a named example as a supporting detail:*

Animal Migration
Animals with No Eyes
Coral Reefs: Colorful Underwater Habitats (SRT)
Countries Around the World: England
Countries Around the World: France
First Nations of North America: Great Basin Indians
Maurice Sendak (Author Biographies)
Meat-Eating Plants and Other Extreme Plant Life
Parks of the U.S.A.
Scaly Blood Squirters and Other Extreme Reptiles
The Lincoln Memorial (American Symbols)
The Story of Corn

Specificity and Proper Nouns (grades 1–4)

Integrate the use of *specificity* with your lessons about nouns, proper nouns, and the convention of capitalizing names. Present models of text that students can revise for specificity and applying capitalization rules. Make *specificity* a function of revision and editing as well as a Target Skill during composing (drafting).

General to Specific

Review the concept of specificity with your students by playing the General-to-Specific Game. You will find a detailed description of this game in Chapter 2, Organizing Informational Writing.

Specificity as a Target Skill

Model *specificity* during composing for your students, and show them how to **revise** existing text to be more specific. When you write in front of your class, think aloud as your revise for *specificity.* For example, write: *My dog is not feeling well. He curls himself up and shivers. I think I ought to take him to the veterinarian in town.* Say, "Oh, my readers might like to know which veterinarian and town." Cross out town. "I am going to change it to *Dr. Goodall, the veterinarian in Bennington.* And why don't I tell what kind of dog I have?" Cross out dog. "I am changing *dog* to *Irish setter.* Now maybe my readers will see better what I mean."

Ask students to listen for people, places, and things that can be more specific, even named, when they hear each other's writing in peer conferences. When they identify a place in the manuscript where they can ask "Can you be more specific?" the author may choose to revise.

C. Presenting Information Graphically (grades K–4)

They say a picture is worth a thousand words. In informational writing, we extend that maxim to include many graphic ways to present bits of information, including labeled photographs, close-ups, far views, diagrams, charts, tables, and graphs. We can cram lots of information into such graphics, helping our readers quickly analyze, compare, discover patterns, make inferences, plan, or summarize.

Capstone mentor texts not only illustrate a variety of graphics, but they provide information that young writers themselves can represent in graphic form. We need to show them how to generate and include graphics in their own informational writing. As children become familiar with how to construct and use graphics, their ability to analyze and interpret them grows proportionately. They become visually literate—a critical skill in this modern information age.

Labeled Photographs, Diagrams, Charts, Graphs, and Maps

The graphic form a writer chooses for presenting information depends on his purpose. Labeled pictures draw attention to specific information. Charts, tables, and graphs, help readers compare and summarize information. Flow diagrams or timelines, help readers follow a sequence.

Before young writers can make decisions about the most appropriate graphic to use in their informational writing, they need to see them constructed, have the opportunity to construct them themselves, and practice interpreting them in informational text. In other words, they must become very familiar with them. The school year offers many opportunities to categorize and list, quantify, compare, and summarize information in graphic form. Look for all the possibilities in your classroom.

- day schedule
- weather record
- calendar of events
- message boards
- organizing materials in the room
- labeling the room
- classroom news
- record keeping: books read, turns taken in an activity
- field trips: data recording forms
- science activities: data gathering, observation and description, categorizing objects, counting
- literature response
- diagrams to accompany directions
- math: counting, graphing, comparing information about people, places, things
- describing sequence in a process: art, social studies, science projects
- making class books

1. Labeled Photographs (grades K–4)

A labeled or captioned photograph is one of the simplest graphic means to direct a reader's attention to information. Photos can be labeled to show named parts of a whole, acting as a picture glossary. They may show different views of the item under study: cross sections, cutaways, magnified close-ups, or panoramic far views. Captions identify or call attention to details in a picture. Be sure to point out to your young writers that captions do not replace writing about a topic, they support it.

Caption Writers

To avoid creating a classroom of caption writers, writers who draw a picture and write a single labeling-type sentence, always model writing of more than one related sentence, and encourage your emergent and young developing writers to do the same.

Capstone nonfiction mentor texts that illustrate *the use of labeled photographs, insets, and close-ups:*

A Bee's Life (SRT)
Animal Spikes and Spines (SRT)
Animals with No Eyes
Communities
Comparing Creatures (SRT)
Coral Reefs: Colorful Underwater Habitats (SRT)
Food from Farms (SRT)
From Mealworm to Beetle (SRT)
Goliath Bird-Eating Spiders and Other Extreme Bugs
If I Were an Astronaut
Life Cycles (Watch It Grow) (SRT)
Magnification
Mapping
Meat-Eating Plants and Other Extreme Plant Life
Stegosaurus: Armored Defender
The Environment Challenge: Bridging the Energy Gap (Express Edition)
The Gettysburg Address in Translation
The Life Cycle of Reptiles
Using Your Senses (SRT)
Weather Watchers: Weather (SRT)
World Cultures

Labels

At the start of the year, give your students the job of labeling the things in the classroom that you usually would label. Take your class on a walk through the school halls, library, and other classrooms to see what information their labels contain. Record the text of labels that the children spot. On your return to the classroom, hold discussions about what the class labels should tell, how big they should be (and why), and how much text to put on them. Help students use letter templates to make labels, or generate large-font labels on the class computer.

Labeled photographs

In a shared reading of **Weather Watchers: Weather,** introduce your young writers to labeled photographs. Provide your kindergarten and first graders with a collection of magazine pictures to label with felt-tipped pens.

After a shared reading of **Animal Spikes and Spines,** have children cut pictures of animals and people from magazines to label with felt-tipped pens. They can label heads with hair, eyes, ears, noses, mouths, arms, legs, fingers, hands, and feet. Make a vocabulary chart of the features they label. Help them trace their own bodies on brown wrapping paper and ask them to draw their faces and label body parts, using the class chart for reference and spelling.

In any shared writing activity, suggest and add a small sketch to the class-generated text and label it. Add labeled sketches to your modeled writing. After activities of this kind, encourage students to use labeled drawings in their independent writing.

Other Views: Close-ups and Far Views (panoramas)

View Scopes: Collect paper towel or bathroom tissue tubes, enough for each student. Demonstrate how to use them as close-up or far-view scopes. Have children stand about six inches from the class United States map and tell how many states they can see through their scope. Then have them stand one foot away and tell how many.

Take children outside to view things on the ground or in the playground, from the top of the slide and from the ground, looking at patterns like the fencing or windows or bricks of the school building, all from close and farther away.

Lead a class discussion about the relationship of how much they can see through the scope to how big things appear.

- The bigger the distance (farther away you are), the bigger an area you can see. The smaller the distance (closer you are), the smaller an area you can see. (In other words, *distance from* and *area seen* are **directly** related.)

- The bigger the distance (farther away you are), the smaller things appear. The smaller the *distance* (closer you are), the bigger things appear (In other words, distance and *size appearance* are **inversely** related.)

Don't be afraid to use these relationship terms with your young students. Find other relationships that can be described as directly or inversely related. Observing and articulating these kinds of logical relationships is a critical thinking skill.

Directly related: (more-more)

The more it rains, the wetter we get.

The more we practice a skill, the better we get at it.

The more acorns there are this fall, the fatter the squirrels will get.

The more kids on a floating raft, the deeper it floats in the water.

Inversely related: (more-less)

The colder it gets, the fewer people come to sit in the park.

The more you spend, the less money you have.

The more we recycle, the less garbage goes in the landfill.

Magnifying Glasses. Introduce your students to magnifying glasses and have them examine science materials, such as rocks, shells, bugs, twigs, bark, leaves, and blossoms. Ask students to draw close-up views of parts of objects. Display their drawings and ask other students to guess what they are.

Drawing and interpreting close-up views is a particularly useful skill in nature study where the finest of details gives us the clues to identifying plants, animals, rocks, fossils, and such. For example, deciduous-tree leaf scars, the scars on twigs left by fallen leaves, show where the veins entered the leaf. The leaf-scar pattern helps identity the tree.

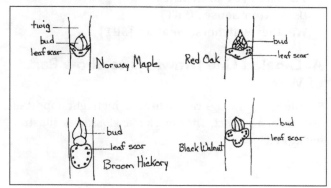

2. Diagrams (grades K–4)

The precursors to diagrams are the labeled pictures emergent writers draw. They use pictures to communicate ideas before they write. As they learn the symbols (letters and blends) that represent the sound of their voices, they begin to label their drawing with the starting consonants of the names of things in the picture. As they learn more symbol-to-sound connections, and begin to use transitional forms of spelling, they tend to write more and draw less.

But many students, with artistic talent and strong visions of their ideas, retain drawing as an integral part of their prewriting and communication. We should encourage young writers in their use of graphics, and teach them further techniques, rather than insist they give up drawing when they have learned to write. We should help them refine their natural skills and show them how to use them to advantage.

Capstone nonfiction mentor texts that illustrate *the use of diagrams:*

A Monarch Butterfly's Journey
Bug Homes
Bug Parts
Bug Senses
Changing Seasons (SRT)
Communities
Comparing Creatures (SRT)
Goliath Bird-Eating Spiders and Other
    Extreme Bugs
Life Cycles (Watch It Grow) (SRT)
Meat-Eating Plants and Other Extreme Plant Life
Monsters of the Deep
Solar Power
The Environment Challenge: Bridging the
    Energy Gap (Express Edition)
The Gettysburg Address in Translation
The Life Cycle of Insects
The Life Cycle of Reptiles
Using Your Senses (SRT)
Weather Watchers: Weather (SRT)

A. Labeled Line Drawings to Show Parts of Whole

Simple line drawings can be used to highlight important aspects of a subject. They work like glossaries, illustrating key terms.

Labeled line drawings are a wonderful way for children to explain what they see or know. Show them diagrams in books and magazines. Model how to draw a simple diagram, such as the parts of a pencil or a classroom plant. Invite students to find objects in the room to draw and label. Those with multiple parts are the ones for which to look. Provide students with natural materials, such as flowers and shells to draw and label. Bring movable toys or a bicycle to your class and have your students make diagrams of them.

Begin using diagrams in various science activities at the same time you focus on descriptive writing, early in the school year. Drawing diagrams takes advantage of children's observational skills, and it nurtures and develops those skills.

Science Study Example

The study of bugs makes a good start to using diagrams in informational text. Bugs are available in most schoolyard environments and children tend to be interested in them. This subject is well supported by the Capstone photo-illustrated science texts: *Bug Babies, Bug Food, Bug Homes, Bug Senses, Bug Parts, A Monarch Butterfly's Journey, The Life Cycle of Insects.* Most of these books include close-up views of insects. Following the model presented in these books, students should draw diagrams of the bugs they study, and include them in their informational writing.

B. Flow Diagrams

Flow diagrams are linear representations of the sequence of steps in a process. They show, through the use of arrows, connecting lines, and numbered sections, how things are linked and ordered, and how they change, move, or develop in the process. Nonfiction writers use them for describing life cycles of plants or animals, progressive changes in a system, how something gets from one place to another, how to make something, cause and effect, and more.

Capstone nonfiction mentor texts that illustrate *cycles:*

A Bee's Life (SRT)
A Monarch Butterfly's Journey
Goliath Bird-Eating Spiders and Other
    Extreme Bugs
Life Cycles (Watch It Grow) (SRT)
Solar Power
The Changing Seasons (SRT)

The Environment Challenge: Bridging the
   Energy Gap (Express Edition)
The Life Cycle of Birds
The Life Cycle of Insects
The Life Cycle of Reptiles

Read *Life Cycles* or *A Monarch Butterfly's Journey* to your class. Discuss life cycles and how they are made up of a sequence of steps. Help your students follow the cycles described in the books, naming the event or what occurs during each step. Explain to your students the difference between a recursive cycle and a linear process. Compare, for instance, the life cycle of insects or frogs versus the process of making a peanut butter sandwich. The linear process has a start and a finish, while a cycle does not. (Which starts the cycle, the chicken or the egg?)

Using one of the titles from the cycles list, model how to draw a life cycle, complete with arrows and labels for all the significant items.

Capstone nonfiction mentor texts that illustrate *processes*:

Flesh-Eating Machines
Mapping
Meat-Eating Plants and Other Extreme Plant Life
Monsters of the Deep
Scaly Blood Squirters and Other Extreme Reptiles
**The Environment Challenge: Bridging the
   Energy Gap (Express Edition)**
Up North and Down South

Using one of the listed titles, model a flow diagram to show linear sequence. Young writers usually like to present the sequence of a process as a series of boxes with a picture drawn in each box while older students will use arrows and lines to connect steps.

Select a process that your students perform and invite them to draw the process in a flow diagram. It will be easier for them to do this if they go through the process and record as they go. Emphasize the inclusion of labels and arrows as a Target Skill. (See page 84 for a student example.)

Integrate the use of labeled drawings and diagrams in writing about science, art, and math. Make diagrams part of the grading rubric for an appropriate informational piece in grades two through four.

C. Map Drawings

Read the primary-level mentor texts, *People in My Neighborhood* or *A Math Hike*, with your students. Show them how a map could be drawn to illustrate the information in the texts: *People in My Neighborhood: next to Lisa's, next door, down the street, at the community center; A Math Hike: the first stop is the pond, look at this tree, in the grass, in the sky.* Use other books, both fiction and nonfiction, to show students how to draw a map of the information in the text.

Other Capstone mentor texts that provide your young writers with material for map-drawing responses are:

- *A Monarch Butterfly's Journey:* Draw a map to show the possible route a Monarch might take from the northeastern United States to Mexico.
- *Animal Migration:* Draw a map of the route of migrating Sand Hill Cranes.
- *The Environment Challenge: Bridging the Energy Gap (Express Edition):* Draw a map showing the countries that have had environmental energy disasters; map out the appliances in your home where you could be saving energy.
- *The Environment Challenge: Avoiding Hunger and Finding Water (Express Edition):* Draw a map of the countries most affected by famine.

Capstone mentor texts that illustrate *maps*:

Ancient Greece: Birthplace of Democracy
Animals in Danger in South America
Are We There Yet?
Coral Reefs: Colorful Underwater Habitats (SRT)
Countries Around the World: England
Countries Around the World: France
First Nations of North America: California Indians
First Nations of North America: Great Basin Indians
Kids' Guide to Government: Local Government
Life Cycle of Fish
Mapping
Oceans
**The Environment Challenge: Avoiding Hunger
   and Finding Water (Express Edition)**
**The Environment Challenge: Bridging the
   Energy Gap (Express Edition)**
**The U.S. Constitution, Bill of Rights,
   and a New Nation**
World Cultures

Fourth grader shows a process described in *Growing Pumpkins*.

3. List: A Simple Chart (grades K–4)

In Chapter 2, Organizing Informational Writing, I discussed listing and its relationship to organizing expository writing. Listing can also be used to graphically present information.

The simplest chart is a list. Lists show categories of information. Categorizing is a critical writing and thinking skill. Kindergarten and first grade teachers find dozens of opportunities for their students to practice this concrete operation. The task requires children to compare things according to an attribute and then sort them into groups of items that share the same attribute.

The most concrete task is comparing objects—toys, math shapes, colored items, pasta, leaves, beads, blocks. Next, more abstract than sorting objects is *sorting pictures of objects.* Finally, more abstract than sorting pictures is sorting *words* that name objects. In all cases, the children should articulate the reason why they place various objects together (categorized them).

Sorting and categorizing activities plus General-to-Specific Games (see pages 23–25, 31) train your young writers to be good list makers. Encourage students to make lists often. The youngest students can make picture or object lists until they can read what they write.

Lists from mentor texts. Students can use most of the Capstone nonfiction texts for sources of lists. Encourage them to use both the text and the photographs as resources for list items. They can add further information from their experience and knowledge. In kindergarten and first grade construct the list during shared reading and shared writing. In higher grades have students work in partnerships or groups to construct lists from the mentor texts they choose. Some examples:

- *Weather Watchers: Weather:* list various kinds of weather
- *Is It Living or Nonliving? Series:* list the attributes of living things or nonliving things
- *Changing Seasons:* list activities for each season
- *Look Inside a Pond:* list animals that live in or near a pond
- *An Illustrated Timeline of U.S. States:* list all the states or list things you know about your home state
- *The Environment Challenge: Bridging the Energy Gap (Express Edition):* list sources of energy
- *The Environment Challenge: Avoiding Hunger and Finding Water (Express Edition):* list the causes of famine and drought

4. Developed Charts or Tables (grades 1–4)

Charts that have multiple columns and rows are called tables or matrices. They help writers present categorized information in multiple lists. They can be used to schedule events, compare, find patterns, and summarize information.

Capstone mentor texts that illustrate the use of charts:

An Illustrated Timeline of U.S. States
Animals in Danger in South America
Changing Seasons (SRT)
Countries Around the World: Afghanistan
Countries Around the World: Costa Rica
Countries Around the World: England
Countries Around the World: France
Countries Around the World: India
First Nations of North America: California Indians
Graphing Immigration
Graphing War and Conflict
Is It Living or Nonliving? Series (SRT)
Look Inside a Pond
Ocean Animal Adaptations (SRT)
Polar Animal Adaptations (SRT)
Rain Forest Animal Adaptations (SRT)
Scaly Blood Squirters and Other Extreme Reptiles
The Environment Challenge: Avoiding Hunger and Finding Water (Express Edition)
The Environment Challenge: Bridging the Energy Gap (Express Edition)
The Life Cycle of Fish
The Life Cycle of Reptiles
Weather Watchers: Weather (SRT)
World Cultures

A. Two-Column Chart

Once young writers are facile with list making, introduce the use of a **two-column chart.** In these side-by-side lists, there are no labeled rows. The items are related vertically, and side-by-side items do not necessarily correspond with one another. See the following Push and Pull chart.

I introduce this lesson in grades one or higher through a science activity using nonfiction informational texts about conductivity, buoyancy (sink or float), dissolve in water or not, forces of push and pull, magnetism, and other variations of *either/or*. After a **shared reading** of such texts, students conduct experiments with these concepts and make two-column data-collecting charts to report their findings.

Kindergarten students often use pictures in place of words in their charts. When students later write about what they did and what they found, they should include the chart in their text—cut and paste the chart in, or draw a smaller version of the chart.

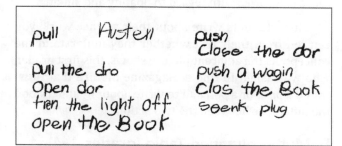

First grader charts his pushes and pulls.

Science Tip

A simple electric circuit can be used to test conductivity: Students either place the object to be tested across the gap in the switch or a gap they make in the circuit.

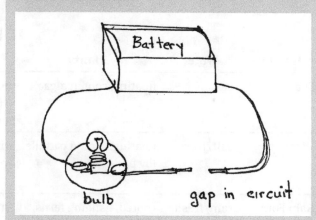

A two-column chart can be created: materials that conduct electricity, materials that don't.

In kindergarten and first grade, build a class chart through a shared writing experience, with students contributing the data from their observations. In higher grades, have your students build the class chart and enter their findings themselves.

Follow with Writing

In primary grades, follow the chart making with shared writing to describe the process; that is, what the students did acting as scientists, and what they discovered. Help them analyze the chart to find categories of materials. Examples: Sink or Float—wooden things, metal things, plastic things, flat things, etc. Ask them what they conclude, or what generalizations they can make about those categories with regard to floating and sinking.

When students write about their science work, you can tell from their text whether they understand the concept. As the adjacent picture shows, this first grader, who was asked to find a magazine picture that illustrated a *push* or a *pull* and to write about it, understood the difference between the two actions.

B. Multi-Columned Table (grades 1–4)

A table with multiple columns and rows can be used to display information about a number of items that share some common attributes. Names of the items are listed along one axis while the attributes, which apply to the items, are listed on the other. A table makes it easy for readers to make comparisons and generalizations.

Capstone mentor texts, such as *Comparing Creatures, Comparing Materials, Desert Animal Adaptations,* and *Look Inside a Pond* are excellent resources to show children how to build a table. The table will help students understand the similarities and differences among these habitats. (See also: Contrast, Chapter 3, Composing Skills.) In the primary grades, you will have to help the children name the attributes or categories as this is an abstract task.

Katelyn

These kittens are pulling on some yarn.

Habitats

Habitat	Water	Plants	Animals	Use to People
Sea	salt	floating, rooted algae	fish, whales, reptiles, shells, coral, plankton, seals, octopus	food, transportation, recreation, rain source, heat source
Wetlands	salt/fresh	floating, rooted cattails, lily pads	fish, birds, mammals, reptiles, insects, crayfish, bears, deer, raccoon	food, recreation, flood control, trap fresh water
Rain Forest	rain/fresh	rooted, hanging ferns, mushrooms, bananas	mammals, birds, reptiles, insects, frogs	food, medicinal plants, dyes, soap, candles, trap fresh water
Pond	fresh	floating/rooted	mammals, birds, reptiles, insects, frogs, moose, raccoon	trap fresh water, food
Tree		fungus, moss	mammals, birds, insects, frogs, reptiles	shade, wood, fruit, nuts, syrup

Use in Writing

Tables are excellent prewriting tools. They can be built as large class charts during a thematic unit. Each day, students can add to the chart as they learn new bits of information. The completed table serves as a word wall for the children to reference when they write about the topic. Developing writers—those that can read what they wrote yesterday—should be responsible for the correct spelling of topic-related words in their writing when those words are displayed on class charts.

Other Capstone titles, sometimes used in combination, can provide the data for a table. Have young writers in third and fourth grade work in teams to build a table from one or more of these books. Encourage teams to create their own headings—to decide on the common attributes of the individual items or animals studied—but you should be prepared to provide help. Included here are some sample column headings.

- *Comparing Creatures:* rows of animals; columns of attributes like size, where they live, what they eat

- *Comparing Materials:* rows of materials; columns of attributes like live or man-made, texture, hardness, uses

- *Countries Around the World: Costa Rica:* rows of regions; columns of attributes like popular industries and climate

- *Countries Around the World: India:* rows of prime ministers; columns of attributes like years served, major changes enacted

- *Desert Animal Adaptations:* rows of animals; columns of adaptations like feeding, ways to cope with heat, movement

In a shared writing experience, build a table that utilizes information from your class science, math, social studies, music, or art activities. You might build one that is based on description, to parallel the study of attributes in writing and science. Or you might build one depicting students' activities and schedules during writing time.

First Graders Using a Table

Kathleen, a first-grade teacher in Jefferson Parish, Louisiana, helps her students organize what they know about a topic as they study it in great detail: reading information and fiction books, watching a film, visiting a website, taking a field trip, doing a hands-on science or art project, talking about pictures, etc. Following a class discussion, Kathleen and her class construct a table that organizes the basic facts about the topic.

For example, when the class studied animals, they listed each animal and recorded similar information about each one. To help them read the table and use it, Kathleen wrote each row in a different color. She wrote cat information in red, dog information in blue, cow information in green, and so forth. Children then chose an animal they wanted to write about. Kathleen encouraged them to use the table and to add any other information they knew.

Animals We Know

Animal	Looks Like	Eats	Noise	Lives	Moves
Cat	furry, pointy ears, whiskers, tail, 4 legs, claws that go back in, paw pads	birds, mice catfood, fish	purr meow growl hiss	in a house	walks climbs slinks pounces
Dog	furry, big teeth, claws that are out, paw pads, tail 4 legs	bones meat Puppy Chow spaghetti	growl bark pant whines	dog house our house	runs walks trots
Cow	big, brown, fur, 4 legs, horns, udder	grass hay	moos	farm ranch	walks drools
Parakeet	2 legs, feathers beak green + blue yellow circle around their eyes	seeds fruit lettuce	screech peep talking	bird cage rain forest	flies hops swoops claws

5. Graphs (grades 1–4)

Graphs quantify information and can be used to make visual comparisons of quantities, record measurements, and answer questions about data. They are more abstract than diagrams and charts. The most concrete, and therefore the place to start with primary students, are bar graphs. They are based on counting. After students understand and can create bar graphs, introduce them to line or pie graphs.

Physical Bar Graphs

Before you ask children to create or interpret bar graphs, demonstrate how to construct physical graphs. These are graphs that children build of the real items to be counted and compared.

Here are some examples of physical graphing.

- **To determine preferences or choices:** Make 6–8-inch body figures of card stock or oak tag for your students. Have them decorate them to represent themselves. Glue small magnets on the back of each. On a daily basis, pose a question to your students that requires them to vote or be counted. Write the choices on the board as a list and have each student place his or her oak-tag figure on the line as a vote for that choice. Students will create a bar graph as they do. (Make sure the figures line up vertically.) Guide students to make summarizing statements about what the graphs shows, i.e., interpret the graph.

A physical graph using a hand to represent a unit.

- **To determine occurrences:** To find out which color M&M or Skittle is the most common in a package, have students fill a series of test tubes in a rack, one for each color candy, to create a physical bar graph. Have them articulate a summary of the data, i.e., interpret the physical graph.

Capstone mentor texts that illustrate *graphs*:

Bar Graphs
Countries Around the World: Afghanistan
Countries Around the World: England
Countries Around the World: France
Countries Around the World: India
Graphing Immigration
Graphing War and Conflict
Graphs
Pictographs
Pie Graphs
Tally Charts
The Environment Challenge: Avoiding Hunger and Finding Water (Express Edition)
The Environment Challenge: Bridging the Energy Gap (Express Edition)

The mentor text *Graphs* illustrates bar graphs and how to construct them. Review the physical graphs that students previously constructed, including each unit's value.

Using an appropriate mentor text as a source of data, help students construct bar graphs. Show them how an author might use such a graph to summarize or illustrate informational text. (For the youngest students, the most difficult task in constructing bar graphs will be labeling the vertical and horizontal axes.)

Use other mentor texts to show students how to construct other simple graphs. Model how to use the graphs to illustrate their information. For instance, if students write about a sample day in their life during the school year, they might summarize the information in a pie graph.

Capstone mentor texts *as data sources for graphing*:

- *Counting at the Parade:* (Kindergarten) Graph of the number of participants/instruments
- *The Story of Corn:* Graph after class survey of favorite corn product (chips, corn dogs, corn bread, etc.)
- *Using Money (SRT):* Graph after class survey of what students use their money for
- *Matter:* Construct graph of quantity of the items in the classroom in the three states of matter: solid, liquid, gas

D. Practice Locating Supporting Details in Nonfiction Text (grades 2–4)

After your students have had practice using supporting details in their own writing, they will start to identify them in professional text. Encourage them to find examples in news and science texts, such as *Scholastic News, Time for Kids, Ranger Rick, National Geographic Kids,* and other science and current event materials, at or below their reading level. (Student analysis of text should always be conducted on easy-to-read material.)

Have the students highlight examples of both written and graphic supporting details in the text. Let them create a color code for the kinds of supporting detail. Example: red for *definition,* green for *specific examples,* yellow for *charts,* blue for *numbers,* etc.

Chapter Summary

Just as the techniques of organizing and composing informational writing employ critical thinking skills (general to specific, sorting and categorizing, comparing, sequencing, noting relationships and patterns) so too does the graphic representation of information and its interpretation. When we teach writing craft using nonfiction mentor texts as models, we have the opportunity to develop important skills all our students can use for life.

Chapter 6: **A Sense of Sentence: Editing by Ear**

Editing prepares a piece of writing for the public by making it conform to conventions of punctuation, capitalization, and spelling. Editing will not improve a poorly written piece that lacks ideas, organization, and effective use of language. But without editing, a well-written piece may be unintelligible.

When I introduce young writers to the importance of editing, I use a spinach-on-your-teeth analogy—if a speaker has spinach on his front teeth, listeners will focus on the spinach, not on what he is saying. Likewise, in writing, readers will focus on convention mistakes rather than on what the writer is saying.

Teach your young writers how to edit by having them:

- edit someone else's writing—it is much easier to find mistakes in another writer's work than in their own,

- edit by ear—use their natural ear for the syntax of language to find end punctuation and the beginning capitalization of the next sentence. (This technique is described in the following subsection.), and

- edit for one convention at a time—read each other's papers several times, once for each convention they know.

Here, I will deal only with editing that you can use Capstone mentor texts to illustrate—end punctuation, capitalization of a starting sentence, and series commas. For information about teaching editing that addresses repetitive phrases, pronouns, or nouns; capitalization; spelling; and such, I refer you to my books, *Teaching the Youngest Writers: A Practical Guide* and *Building a Writing Community: A Practical Guide*.

Sentence End Punctuation and Capitalization

The earliest editing skill you can teach young writers is editing for end punctuation. (I include capitalizing the start of sentences in this lesson as well.) I teach young writers that it is easier to hear where end punctuation belongs than to see where it belongs.

Chomsky's research[1] in the 1950s tells us that children acquire the syntax of their native language in the early months of infancy; they are born with the ability to do so. By the time they reach school age, they understand the complexities and nuances of the language in which they have been raised. It is this understanding that makes *Editing by Ear* possible and effective.

Have you ever seen Victor Borge, comedian-pianist, perform his oral-punctuation routine? He reads a short selection of prose, using an array of vocal sounds and accompanying hand gestures to indicate each of the punctuation marks required. The prose is filled with every punctuation known to mankind, and his sounds and gestures are hilarious. Borge's routine can be adapted as a model for Editing by Ear.

Editing-by-Ear Model (grades K–4)

The Editing-by-Ear model takes approximately 25 minutes. Repeat it often as a starting component to daily writing workshop.

Kindergarten

In kindergarten use this model for emergent writers who understand the message principle, i.e., that what they say can be written on paper, and who are using starting and ending consonants for words or are using transitional spelling. Even if they cannot reread their message at a later time because they are not truly decoding, they can still profit from this model.

---

[1]Noam Chomsky, *Syntactic Structures* (Mouton, 1957)

You will need:

- a Capstone mentor text in Shared Reading Text format (Use one that you have used previously for its science content. Use one in which the end-punctuation marks you want to feature—period, question mark, exclamation mark—predominate.)

- the Author's Chair

- an easel and a pointer

- a small metal clicker (See Bibliography for an Internet source of inexpensive clickers.)

- a writer who can read his or her own writing consisting of two or more sentences

a) Gather the class to read *chorally* with you from the Shared Reading Text. Read the first sentence. Then invite students to say or read it with you. Continue with the rest of the text, modeling expressive reading. Encourage your students to mimic your voice. Have them listen for the slight voice drop at the end of declarative sentences.

In subsequent models ask first, second, and third graders to listen for the rise in volume for exclamations, and the rise in pitch and the pause for questions. After each sentence, point to the end-punctuation mark. Often, a student will announce that the next sentence starts with a capital letter. If no one does, prompt your students by asking what they notice about the start of the next sentence.

b) Continue with the choral reading until your young writers understand the connection between the end punctuation and the corresponding voice inflections. (Choral reading reinforces the *sound* of sentences. Use it often with your primary students.)

c) Now, take the Shared Reading Text from the easel and read the remainder of the text to the class. Give the Editing Clicker to a student and ask her to click when she **hears** the end of a sentence. Children will take turns using the clicker. Ask the rest of the class to snap their fingers or cluck with their tongues when they **hear** the end of a sentence. (Of course, they will all cluck or snap for a minute or two. Expect it.) Children enjoy making up new sounds for the additional punctuation marks of a question or exclamation mark.

d) Finally, tell them you are going to try to trick them and they will need to listen carefully to your voice. Read part of a sentence, suspending your voice. Example: *A wetland habitat is home to many kinds...* Stop there and look up. Several children will have clucked but most will be looking expectantly at you to complete the sentence. Ask, "Are you waiting to hear 'many kinds of what?' Sure. I didn't finish the sentence, did I?"

e) Finish the book with the text revealed and have young writers continue to read chorally, mimicking you and clicking and clucking the end punctuation.

In kindergarten classes, you should stop the model here. Repeat it several times in the future. In both kindergarten and first grade, *make the sound of a period,* a cluck or a snap, as you write during shared or modeled writing. Encourage children to do the same when they write.

A primary teacher told me she had a visitor to the class during the independent writing component of her writing workshop. After a few moments, the visitor came to her with a puzzled expression and whispered, "Why are some of them clucking their tongues?" The teacher got a kick out of explaining how children *punctuate* their writing in her first grade class.

---

f) When the choral reading is finished in your **first or second grade** class, invite the young writer to read his or her piece from the Author's Chair while classmates click, snap, or cluck as they hear the ends of sentences. The writer may add punctuation and capitalization he or she may have left out.

- In first grade and above, invite students to try Editing by Ear in peer partnerships. Have them pre-read their pieces so they can read them smoothly and with expression. When they read to their partners, the listeners will sound the signal for end punctuation, and may ask the writers if they started the following sentences with capital letters.

- Do not expect young writers to perform Editing by Ear accurately the first few times. Some young writers will have incomplete sentences and read them incorrectly. Other children will *call* the words, stopping at the end of a line instead of the end of a sentence. They are still working on decoding the words and may not be able to read with expression. Their partner won't know what to do. Rove around helping and encouraging the partnerships.

- Afterward, ask the positive "Who found places that they could clap or cluck?" rather than the negative "Who forgot to add a period?" Praise each successful listening editor.

- For reinforcement, have students read simple classroom texts to each other, emphasizing that the Target Skill is to read with expression. Have each listener give the sound signals for the end punctuation they hear. (Peer pairs may use the class editing clickers for this activity.) Continue to make sound signals for end punctuation when you model writing for your students.

Capstone mentor texts to use for *Editing-by-Ear lessons:*

Periods
Every Capstone mentor text

Exclamation Marks
Animals in Danger in South America
Animals with No Eyes
Fun at the Zoo
Let's Move
Show Me the United States
Which Seed Is This? (SRT)
Who Really Created Democracy?

Questions
Animals with No Eyes
Desert Animal Adaptations
Fun at the Zoo
Polar Animal Adaptations (SRT)
Show Me the U.S. Presidency
Who Really Created Democracy?

Additional Editing by Ear (grades 2–5)

The same editing-by-ear model can be used to help students punctuate lists with series commas. The suspension and rise in your voice is very obvious when you read a list within a sentence. Encourage students to use lists within their writing, as a Target Skill, to practice the punctuation.

Series Commas
Ancient China: Beyond the Great Wall
Ancient Greece: Birthplace of Democracy
Animal Migration
Animals in Danger in South America
Animals with No Eyes
Life Cycles (Watch It Grow) (SRT)
Look Inside a Tree
Parks of the U.S.A.
Rain Forest Animal Adaptations (SRT)
Which Seed Is This? (SRT)
Who Really Discovered America?

After taking part in repetitive editing-by-ear models, practicing choral reading, and using sound signals in peer editing conferences, most elementary students learn to punctuate their own sentences. A second-grade teacher who uses this technique extensively told me her students come to her and say, "May we have the class clicker? We want to edit our papers."

Bibliography

Recommended Reading

Achieve, Inc. Next Generation Science Standards. Washington, DC: Achieve, Inc., 2013.

Ackerman, Diane. *A Natural History of the Senses.* New York: Random House, 1990.

Freeman, Marcia S. *Building a Writing Community: A Practical Guide.* Gainesville: Maupin House Publishing, 1995.

Freeman, Marcia S. *Listen to This: Developing an Ear for Expository.* Gainesville: Maupin House Publishing, 1997.

Freeman, Marcia S. *Models for Teaching Writing-Craft Target Skills.* Gainesville: Maupin House Publishing, 2005.

Freeman, Marcia S. *Teaching the Youngest Writers: A Practical Guide.* Gainesville: Maupin House Publishing, 1998.

Moline, Steve. *I See What You Mean: Children at Work with Visual Information.* York: Stenhouse Publishers, 1995.

National Governors Association Center for Best Practices & Council of Chief State School Officers. Common Core State Standards. Washington, DC: Authors, 2010.

Provost, Gary. *100 Ways to Improve Your Writing.* New York: New American Library, 1985.

Trussell-Cullen, Alan. *Starting with the Real World.* Carlsbad: Domine Press, 1999.

Zinsser, William. *Writing to Learn.* New York: Harper & Row Publishers, 1988.

Children's Books Cited

Christelow, Eileen. *Five Little Monkeys Jumping on the Bed,* New York: Clarion Books, 1991.

DePaola, Tomie. *Charlie Needs a Cloak.* New York: Simon and Shuster, 1973.

Dragonwagon, Crescent. *All the Awake Animals Are Almost Asleep.* New York: Little, Brown Books, 2012.

Fletcher, Ralph. *Twilight Comes Twice,* New York: Clarion Books, 1997.

Hanson, Joan. *More Similes: Roar Like a Lion As Loud As Thunder and Other "Like" or "As" Comparisons Between Unlike Things.* Minneapolis: Lerner Publications, 1979.

Juster, Norton. *AS: A Surfeit of Similes.* New York: Morrow Junior Books, 1989.

Kellogg, Steven. *Aster Aardvark's Alphabet Adventures.* New York: Morton, 1987.

Moore, Eva. *Lucky Ducklings.* New York: Orchard Books, 2013.

Odom, Melissa W. *A Medal for Murphy.* Gretna: Pelican Publishers, 1987.

Paschkis, Julie. *Play All Day.* Boston: Little, Brown and Company, 1988.

Potter, Beatrix. *The Tale of Mrs. Tittlemouse.* London, Eng.: Frederick Warne, 1910.

Schrecengost, Maity. *Tasso of Tarpon Springs.* Gainesville: Maupin House Publishing, 1998.

Smith, Maggie. *Pigs in Pajamas.* New York: Alfred A. Knopf, 2012.

Spier, Peter. *Crash! Bang! Boom!* Garden City: Doubleday and Company, 1972.

Spier, Peter. *Gobble, Growl, Grunt.* Garden City: Doubleday and Company, 1971.

Steig, William. *The Toy Brother.* New York: HarperCollins, 1996.

Terban, Marvin. *It Figures!: Fun Figures of Speech.* New York: Clarion Books, 1993.

Wood, Audrey. *Quick as a Cricket.* Boston: Houghton Mifflin, 1996.

Material Sources

Editing-by-Ear punctuation clickers: www.sitstay.com (dog obedience website)

Capstone Nonfiction Mentor Text Titles

*SRT = Shared Reading Text

A Baby Rabbit Story (SRT)
A Baby Sea Otter Story (SRT)
A Bee's Life (SRT)
A Math Hike
A Monarch Butterfly's Journey
A Visit to the Airport
All about Boats
All about Snakes and Lizards
An Illustrated Timeline of U.S. States
Ancient China: Beyond the Great Wall
Ancient Greece: Birthplace of Democracy
Animal Migration
Animals in Danger in South America
Animal Spikes and Spines (SRT)
Animals with No Eyes
Are We There Yet?
Bar Graphs
Big, Bigger, Biggest
Bread around the World
Bug Babies
Bug Food
Bug Homes
Bug Parts
Bug Senses
Built from Stone
Changing Seasons (SRT)
Communities
Community Helpers
Comparing Creatures (SRT)
Comparing Materials (SRT)
Cooking Pancakes
Coral Reefs: Colorful Underwater Habitats (SRT)
Counting at the Parade
Countries Around the World: Afghanistan
Countries Around the World: Brazil
Countries Around the World: Chile
Countries Around the World: Costa Rica
Countries Around the World: Czech Republic
Countries Around the World: England
Countries Around the World: France

Countries Around the World: India
Countries Around the World: Iran
Countries Around the World: Scotland
Crystals
Deserts
Desert Animal Adaptations
Desert Seasons
Everybody Moves
Finding Patterns
First Nations of North America: Arctic Peoples
First Nations of North America: California Indians
First Nations of North America: Great Basin Indians
First Nations of North America: Northeast Indians
Flesh-Eating Machines
Food from Farms (SRT)
Food Technology
Fossils
From Egg to Snake
From Mealworm to Beetle (SRT)
Fun at the Zoo
Getting There
Giraffes (SRT)
Goliath Bird-Eating Spiders and Other Extreme Bugs
Graphing Immigration
Graphing War and Conflict
Graphs
Grasslands
Healthy Eating
I Can Help
If I Were an Astronaut
If I Were a Veterinarian
If I Were the President
If the Shoe Fits
Instruments and Music
Inventions
Is It Living or Nonliving? Series (SRT)
Kids' Guide to Government: Local Government
Leading the Way
Lend a Hand
Let's Move
Let's Rock: Crystals

Let's Rock: Fossils
Let's Rock: Metamorphic Rocks
Life Cycles (Watch It Grow) (SRT)
Life in the Time of Abraham Lincoln and the Civil War
Light and Dark (SRT)
Lightning
Long and Short (SRT)
Look and Learn
Look Inside a Pond
Look Inside a Tree
Magnetism: A Question and Answer Book
Magnification
Making Maple Syrup
Mapping
Mapping Your Community
Matter
Maurice Sendak (Author Biographies)
Measure for Measure
Meat-Eating Plants and Other Extreme Plant Life
Monsters of the Deep
Ocean Animal Adaptations (SRT)
Oceans
One Land, Many Cultures
Oranges: From Fruit to Juice
Our Five Senses
Our Global Community (SRT)
Parks of the U.S.A.
People in My Neighborhood
Pictographs
Pie Graphs
Polar Animal Adaptations (SRT)
Pushes and Pulls
Rain (Weather Basics) (SRT)
Rain Forest Animal Adaptations (SRT)
Rain Forests: Gardens of Green (SRT)
Rocks and Minerals
Save the Animals
Scaly Blood Squirters and Other Extreme Reptiles
Science Measurements
Science Tools
Show Me the U.S. Presidency
Show Me the United States
Simply Science
Soil
Solar Power
Stegosaurus: Armored Defender
Storm Tracker: Measuring and Forecasting
Tally Charts
The Attractive Truth about Magnetism
The Bill of Rights
The Bloody, Rotten Roman Empire
The Changing Seasons (SRT)

The Crude, Unpleasant Age of Pirates
The Dreadful, Smelly Colonies
The Environment Challenge: Avoiding Hunger and Finding Water (Express Edition)
The Environment Challenge: Bridging the Energy Gap (Express Edition)
The Gettysburg Address in Translation
The Life Cycle of Birds
The Life Cycle of Fish
The Life Cycle of Insects
The Life Cycle of Reptiles
The Lincoln Memorial (American Symbols)
The Story of Corn
The Terrible, Awful Civil War
The U.S. Constitution, Bill of Rights, and a New Nation
The U.S. Supreme Court (American Symbols)
Then and Now
To Fly in the Sky
Tundras
Up North and Down South
Using Money (SRT)
Using Your Senses (SRT)
Warning: Extreme Weather
Water: Up, Down, and All Around
Weather Watchers: Weather (SRT)
Welcome to Mexico
Welcome to North America
What Did the Aztecs Do for Me?
What Did the Vikings Do for Me?
What Is a Community? (SRT)
What Is a Family? (SRT)
Where People Live
Which Seed Is This? (SRT)
Who Reached the South Pole First?
Who Really Created Democracy?
Who Really Discovered America?
World Cultures
You Can Write an Amazing Journal
Your Five Senses

Recommended Series
Animal Adaptations (A+ Books)
Comparing Bugs (Acorn Read Alouds)
Countries Around the World
Fact Finders: Extreme Life
First Facts
First Nations of North America
Life Cycles (Heinemann Raintree)
Look Inside ... (Heinemann First Library)
Nature Starts (A+ Books—Shared Reading Texts)
Pebble Books: Baby Animals
Wonder Readers (Fluent Level)

Master List of Mentor Texts and Skills

ORGANIZATIONAL

General-to-Specific Scheme
- Animal Migration
- Big, Bigger, Biggest
- Bread Around the World
- Everybody Moves
- Getting There
- Leading the Way
- Our Five Senses
- Parks of the U.S.A.
- Save the Animals
- Science Measurements
- The Bill of Rights
- Weather Watchers: Weather (SRT)

Natural Divisions within a Topic
- All about Boats
- Animal Migration
- Mapping Your Community
- Ocean Animal Adaptations (SRT)
- Oranges: From Fruit to Juice
- Rain Forest Animal Adaptations (SRT)
- The Changing Seasons (SRT)
- The Life Cycle of Birds
- Using Your Senses (SRT)
- Where People Live

Divisions Based on Time
- A Bee's Life (SRT)
- Desert Seasons
- Fossils
- From Egg to Snake
- If the Shoe Fits
- To Fly in the Sky
- Who Reached the South Pole First?

Divisions Based on Place
- Animals with No Eyes
- Look Inside a Tree
- Monsters of the Deep

Steps in a Process
- Cooking Pancakes
- Making Maple Syrup
- Oranges: From Fruit to Juice
- You Can Write an Amazing Journal

COMPOSING

DESCRIPTION

Describing with Verbs
- Animals with No Eyes
- Coral Reefs: Colorful Underwater Habitats (SRT)
- Countries Around the World: Brazil
- Countries Around the World: Chile
- Countries Around the World: Czech Republic
- Flesh-Eating Machines
- From Mealworm to Beetle (SRT)
- Let's Rock: Metamorphic Rocks
- Look Inside a Tree
- Meat-Eating Plants and Other Extreme Plant Life
- Ocean Animal Adaptations (SRT)
- Polar Animal Adaptations (SRT)
- Rain Forest Animal Adaptations (SRT)
- The Story of Corn
- Tundras
- Which Seed Is This? (SRT)

Descriptive Attributes and Adjectives
- A Baby Rabbit Story (SRT)
- A Baby Sea Otter Story (SRT)
- Animals with No Eyes
- Coral Reefs: Colorful Underwater Habitats (SRT)
- Countries Around the World: Costa Rica
- Countries Around the World: India
- Countries Around the World: Iran
- Desert Animal Adaptations
- Flesh-Eating Machines
- Look Inside a Tree
- Meat-Eating Plants and Other Extreme Plant Life

- Ocean Animal Adaptations (SRT)
  - Polar Animal Adaptations (SRT)
  - Using Your Senses (SRT)
  - Which Seed Is This? (SRT)

Descriptive Comparisons
- All about Boats
- Big, Bigger, Biggest
- Countries Around the World: Costa Rica
- Countries Around the World: India
- Countries Around the World: Iran
- Desert Animal Adaptations
- From Mealworm to Beetle (SRT)
- Long and Short (SRT)
- Polar Animal Adaptations (SRT)
- The Attractive Truth about Magnetism
- Welcome to Mexico
- Which Seed Is This? (SRT)

Contrasts and Opposites
- Comparing Materials (SRT)
- Coral Reefs: Colorful Underwater Habitats (SRT)
- Countries Around the World: Costa Rica
- First Nations of North America: Northeast Indians
- Instruments and Music
- Let's Rock: Crystals
- Polar Animal Adaptations (SRT)
- The Terrible, Awful Civil War
- Using Your Senses (SRT)
- Weather Watchers: Weather (SRT)
- Welcome to Mexico
- What Is a Community? (SRT)
- What Is a Family? (SRT)

ENGAGING THE READER
- All about Boats
- Animals with No Eyes
- Community Helpers
- Fun at the Zoo
- Magnetism: A Question and Answer Book
- Meat-Eating Plants and Other Extreme Plant Life
- Parks of the U.S.A.
- Polar Animal Adaptations (SRT)
- The Bloody, Rotten Roman Empire
- The Dreadful, Smelly Colonies
- The Terrible, Awful Civil War
- Up North and Down South
- Using Your Senses (SRT)
- Weather (SRT)

ALLITERATION
- Animal Migration
- Countries Around the World: Costa Rica
- Desert Animal Adaptations
- First Nations of North America: Great Basin Indians
- Flesh-Eating Machines
- Let's Rock: Fossils
- Look Inside a Tree
- Ocean Animal Adaptations (SRT)
- Polar Animal Adaptations (SRT)
- The Crude, Unpleasant Age of Pirates
- The Life Cycle of Birds

SENTENCE VARIATION

Where
- All about Snakes and Lizards
- Built from Stone
- Coral Reefs: Colorful Underwater Habitats (SRT)
- Electricity All Around
- I Can Help
- Let's Rock: Metamorphic Rocks
- Look Inside a Tree
- Rain (Weather Basics) (SRT)
- Tundras
- Which Seed Is This? (SRT)

When
- Built from Stone
- Look Inside a Tree
- Polar Animal Adaptations (SRT)
- Then and Now
- Tundras
- Welcome to North America
- Which Seed Is This? (SRT)

How
- Coral Reefs: Colorful Underwater Habitats (SRT)
- Let's Rock: Metamorphic Rocks
- Look and Learn
- Look Inside a Tree
- The Bloody, Rotten Roman Empire
- Tundras
- Welcome to North America
- Which Seed Is This? (SRT)

Why
- All about Snakes and Lizards
- Animals in Danger in South America
- Animal Spikes and Spines (SRT)
- Built from Stone

- Coral Reefs: Colorful Underwater Habitats (SRT)
- First Nations of North America: Northeast Indians
- Food from Farms (SRT)
- Look Inside a Tree
- Polar Animal Adaptations (SRT)
- The Bloody, Rotten Roman Empire
- Welcome to North America

BEGINNINGS

Question
- Animal Migration
- Countries Around the World: Czech Republic
- Countries Around the World: Scotland
- First Nations of North America: Great Basin Indians
- Fun at the Zoo
- Goliath Bird-Eating Spiders and Other Extreme Bugs
- Oceans
- Storm Tracker: Measuring and Forecasting
- The Dreadful, Smelly Colonies
- The Environment Challenge: Bridging the Energy Gap (Express Edition)
- The Terrible, Awful Civil War
- Weather Watchers: Weather (SRT)

Exclamation
- Fun at the Zoo
- Giraffes (SRT)
- Polar Animal Adaptations (SRT)
- The Bloody, Rotten Roman Empire
- Tundras
- Welcome to Mexico

Talking Directly to the Reader
- A Monarch Butterfly's Journey
- Animals in Danger in South America
- Animals with No Eyes
- Coral Reefs: Colorful Underwater Habitats (SRT)
- Countries Around the World: Chile
- Countries Around the World: Czech Republic
- Meat-Eating Plants and Other Extreme Plant Life
- Monsters of the Deep
- Rain Forests: Gardens of Green (SRT)
- The Attractive Truth about Magnetism
- The Bloody, Rotten Roman Empire
- The Dreadful, Smelly Colonies
- The Terrible, Awful Civil War

Definition
- Community Helpers
- Crystals
- Deserts
- Grasslands
- Oceans
- The Environment Challenge: Bridging the Energy Gap (Express Edition)
- The Life Cycle of Birds
- The U.S. Supreme Court (American Symbols)
- Welcome to Mexico
- Which Seed Is This? (SRT)

Setting
- Ancient Greece: Birthplace of Democracy
- Animals with No Eyes
- Lightning
- Monsters of the Deep
- Scaly Blood Squirters and Other Extreme Reptiles
- The Bloody, Rotten Roman Empire
- The U.S. Constitution, Bill of Rights, and a New Nation
- What Did the Aztecs Do for Me?
- What Did the Vikings Do for Me?

Onomatopoeia
- If I Were a Veterinarian
- Meat-Eating Plants and Other Extreme Plant Life
- Polar Animal Adaptations (SRT)
- The Crude, Unpleasant Age of Pirates
- Water: Up, Down, and All Around

ENDINGS

Universal Word
- Bread around the World
- Finding Patterns
- Grasslands
- Lend a Hand
- Measure for Measure
- Oceans
- Our Global Community (SRT)
- The Terrible, Awful Civil War
- Tundras

Ask the Reader a Question
- All about Snakes and Lizards
- Animals with No Eyes
- Community Helpers
- Rain Forest Animal Adaptations (SRT)
- The Attractive Truth about Magnetism

- The Environment Challenge: Bridging the Energy Gap (Express Edition)
- Using Your Senses (SRT)
- Weather Watchers: Weather (SRT)
- Welcome to Mexico
- You Can Write an Amazing Journal

The Final Step in a Sequence
- A Monarch Butterfly's Journey
- Ancient Greece: Birthplace of Democracy
- Cooking Pancakes
- Mapping
- Who Really Created Democracy?
- Who Really Discovered America?

Exclamations
- All about Boats
- Cooking Pancakes
- Fun at the Zoo
- Graphs
- If I Were the President
- If the Shoe Fits
- Ocean Animal Adaptations (SRT)
- Oranges: From Fruit to Juice
- The Bloody, Rotten Roman Empire
- The Crude, Unpleasant Age of Pirates
- The Dreadful, Smelly Colonies
- Then and Now

Circling Back to the Hook
- Desert Animal Adaptations
- If the Shoe Fits
- Inventions
- Look and Learn
- The Crude, Unpleasant Age of Pirates
- Who Really Created Democracy?
- Who Really Discovered America?

Summarizing
- Coral Reefs: Colorful Underwater Habitats (SRT)
- Look Inside a Pond
- Polar Animal Adaptations (SRT)
- Science Tools
- The Crude, Unpleasant Age of Pirates
- The Lincoln Memorial (American Symbols)
- The Story of Corn
- The Terrible, Awful Civil War
- The U.S. Constitution, Bill of Rights, and a New Nation
- Which Seed Is This? (SRT)

SUPPORTING DETAILS FROM PICTURES
- Healthy Eating
- Mapping Your Community
- Pushes and Pulls
- Life in the Time of Abraham Lincoln and the Civil War

SUPPORTING DETAILS IN TEXT

Specific Examples
- Animals in Danger in South America
- Animals with No Eyes
- Comparing Materials (SRT)
- Coral Reefs: Colorful Underwater Habitats (SRT)
- Countries Around the World: England
- Countries Around the World: France
- Desert Animal Adaptations
- First Nations of North America: California Indians
- Life Cycles (Watch It Grow) (SRT)
- One Land, Many Cultures
- Parks of the U.S.A.
- Polar Animal Adaptations (SRT)
- Rocks and Minerals
- Simply Science
- The Life Cycle of Birds
- Tundras
- Warning: Extreme Weather
- Weather Watchers: Weather (SRT)

Definitions
- Animal Spikes and Spines (SRT)
- Animals with No Eyes
- Built from Stone
- Coral Reefs: Colorful Underwater Habitats (SRT)
- First Nations of North America: Arctic Peoples
- First Nations of North America: Northeast Indians
- Food Technology
- Fun at the Zoo
- Goliath Bird-Eating Spiders and Other Extreme Bugs
- If the Shoe Fits
- Life Cycles (Watch It Grow) (SRT)
- Meat-Eating Plants and other Extreme Plant Life
- Oceans
- Polar Animal Adaptations (SRT)
- Soil
- The Crude, Unpleasant Age of Pirates
- The Environment Challenge: Bridging the Energy Gap (Express Edition)
- Weather Watchers: Weather (SRT)
- Welcome to Mexico
- What Is a Family? (SRT)

Numbers

- Ancient Greece: Birthplace of Democracy
- Animals with No Eyes
- Coral Reefs: Colorful Underwater Habitats (SRT)
- Countries Around the World: England
- Countries Around the World: France
- First Nations of North America: California Indians
- First Nations of North America: Great Basin Indians
- From Egg to Snake
- From Mealworm to Beetle (SRT)
- Let's Rock: Metamorphic Rocks
- Look Inside a Tree
- Parks of the U.S.A.
- Polar Animal Adaptations (SRT)
- The Lincoln Memorial (American Symbols)
- Which Seed Is This? (SRT)

Reasons Why

- Animals in Danger in South America
- Animal Spikes and Spines (SRT)
- Coral Reefs: Colorful Underwater Habitats (SRT)
- Goliath Bird-Eating Spiders and Other Extreme Bugs
- Look Inside a Tree
- Meat-Eating Plants and Other Extreme Plant Life
- The Crude, Unpleasant Age of Pirates
- The Environment Challenge: Bridging the Energy Gap (Express Edition)
- The Life Cycle of Birds
- Welcome to Mexico
- Which Seed Is This? (SRT)

Named Examples (Specificity)

- Animal Migration
- Animals with No Eyes
- Coral Reefs: Colorful Underwater Habitats (SRT)
- Countries Around the World: England
- Countries Around the World: France
- First Nations of North America: Great Basin Indians
- Maurice Sendak (Author Biographies)
- Meat-Eating Plants and Other Extreme Plant Life
- Parks of the U.S.A.
- Scaly Blood Squirters and Other Extreme Reptiles
- The Lincoln Memorial (American Symbols)
- The Story of Corn

PRESENTING INFORMATION GRAPHICALLY

Labeled Photographs, Insets, and Close-ups

- A Bee's Life (SRT)
- Animal Spikes and Spines (SRT)
- Animals with No Eyes
- Communities
- Comparing Creatures (SRT)
- Coral Reefs: Colorful Underwater Habitats (SRT)
- Food from Farms (SRT)
- From Mealworm to Beetle (SRT)
- Goliath Bird-Eating Spiders and Other Extreme Bugs
- If I Were an Astronaut
- Life Cycles (Watch It Grow) (SRT)
- Magnification
- Mapping
- Meat-Eating Plants and Other Extreme Plant Life
- Stegosaurus: Armored Defender
- The Environment Challenge: Bridging the Energy Gap (Express Edition)
- The Gettysburg Address in Translation
- The Life Cycle of Reptiles
- Using Your Senses (SRT)
- Weather Watchers: Weather (SRT)
- World Cultures

Diagrams

- A Monarch Butterfly's Journey
- Bug Homes
- Bug Parts
- Bug Senses
- Changing Seasons (SRT)
- Communities
- Comparing Creatures (SRT)
- Goliath Bird-Eating Spiders and Other Extreme Bugs
- Life Cycles (Watch It Grow) (SRT)
- Meat-Eating Plants and Other Extreme Plant Life
- Monsters of the Deep
- Solar Power
- The Environment Challenge: Bridging the Energy Gap (Express Edition)
- The Gettysburg Address in Translation
- The Life Cycle of Insects
- The Life Cycle of Reptiles
- Using Your Senses (SRT)
- Weather Watchers: Weather (SRT)

Cycles
- A Bee's Life (SRT)
- A Monarch Butterfly's Journey
- Goliath Bird-Eating Spiders and Other Extreme Bugs
- Life Cycles (Watch It Grow) (SRT)
- Solar Power
- The Changing Seasons (SRT)
- The Environment Challenge: Bridging the Energy Gap (Express Edition)
- The Life Cycle of Birds
- The Life Cycle of Insects
- The Life Cycle of Reptiles

Processes
- Flesh-Eating Machines
- Mapping
- Meat-Eating Plants and Other Extreme Plant Life
- Monsters of the Deep
- Scaly Blood Squirters and Other Extreme Reptiles
- The Environment Challenge: Bridging the Energy Gap (Express Edition)
- Up North and Down South

Map Drawings
- A Math Hike
- A Monarch Butterfly's Journey
- Animal Migration
- Countries Around the World: England
- Countries Around the World: France
- First Nations of North America: California Indians
- First Nations of North America: Great Basin Indians
- Kids' Guide to Government: Local Government
- Mapping
- People in My Neighborhood
- The Environment Challenge: Bridging the Energy Gap (Express Edition)
- The Environment Challenge: Avoiding Hunger and Finding Water (Express Edition)
- World Cultures
- Your Five Senses

Lists/Simple Charts
- An Illustrated Timeline of U.S. States
- Changing Seasons (SRT)
- Is It Living or Nonliving? Series (SRT)
- Look Inside a Pond
- The Environment Challenge: Avoiding Hunger and Finding Water (Express Edition)
- The Environment Challenge: Bridging the Energy Gap (Express Edition)
- Weather Watchers: Weather (SRT)

Developed Charts or Tables
- An Illustrated Timeline of U.S. States
- Animals in Danger in South America
- Changing Seasons (SRT)
- Comparing Creatures (SRT)
- Comparing Materials (SRT)
- Countries Around the World: Afghanistan
- Countries Around the World: Costa Rica
- Countries Around the World: England
- Countries Around the World: France
- Countries Around the World: India
- Desert Animal Adaptations
- First Nations of North America: California Indians
- Graphing Immigration
- Graphing War and Conflict
- Is It Living or Nonliving? Series (SRT)
- Look Inside a Pond
- Ocean Animal Adaptations (SRT)
- Polar Animal Adaptations (SRT)
- Rain Forest Animal Adaptations (SRT)
- Scaly Blood Squirters and Other Extreme Reptiles
- The Environment Challenge: Avoiding Hunger and Finding Water (Express Edition)
- The Environment Challenge: Bridging the Energy Gap (Express Edition)
- The Life Cycle of Fish
- The Life Cycle of Reptiles
- Weather Watchers: Weather (SRT)
- World Cultures

Graphs
- Bar Graphs
- Countries Around the World: Afghanistan
- Countries Around the World: England
- Countries Around the World: France
- Countries Around the World: India
- Graphing Immigration
- Graphing War and Conflict
- Graphs
- Pictographs
- Pie Graphs
- Tally Charts
- The Environment Challenge: Avoiding Hunger and Finding Water (Express Edition)
- The Environment Challenge: Bridging the Energy Gap (Express Edition)

EDITING BY EAR

Exclamation Marks
- Animals in Danger in South America
- Animals with No Eyes
- Fun at the Zoo
- Let's Move
- Show Me the United States
- Which Seed Is This? (SRT)
- Who Really Created Democracy?

Questions
- Animals with No Eyes
- Desert Animal Adaptations
- Fun at the Zoo
- Polar Animal Adaptations (SRT)
- Show Me the U.S. Presidency
- Who Really Created Democracy?

Series Commas
- Ancient China: Beyond the Great Wall
- Ancient Greece: Birthplace of Democracy
- Animal Migration
- Animals in Danger in South America
- Animals with No Eyes
- Life Cycles (Watch It Grow) (SRT)
- Look Inside a Tree
- Parks of the U.S.A.
- Rain Forest Animal Adaptations (SRT)
- Which Seed Is This? (SRT)
- Who Really Discovered America?

Index